Japandi Des Beginne s.

The Subtle Art of Japanese & Scandinavian Living

Olivia Wilson

Copyright © 2024 by Olivia Wilson

ISBN: 9798325453861

All rights reserved. No part of this book may be reproduced, stored in a retrieval system, or transmitted in any form or by any means, electronic, mechanical, photocopying, recording, or otherwise, without the prior written permission of the publisher.

CONTENTS

CHAPTER 1: INTRODUCTION TO JAPANDI STYLE 8

CHAPTER 2: JAPANESE & SCANDINAVIAN INFLUENCES 19

CHAPTER 3: ESSENTIAL ELEMENTS OF JAPANDI STYLE..........................29

CHAPTER 4: COLOR PALETTE & TEXTURES 38

CHAPTER 5: FURNITURE & FURNISHINGS 44

CHAPTER 6: SPATIAL LAYOUT & ORGANIZATION 61

CHAPTER 7: LIGHTING DESIGN 66

CHAPTER 8: DECORATIVE ACCENTS & ACCESSORIES.............................73

CHAPTER 9: JAPANDI STYLE IN DIFFERENT ROOMS 79

CHAPTER 10: BRINGING JAPANDI STYLE INTO YOUR HOME 92

CHAPTER 11: INSPIRATIONAL SPACES 97

CHAPTER 12: EMBRACING JAPANDI STYLE IN YOUR LIFE 104

RECOMMENDED RESOURCES 108

Imagine walking into a room where you instantly felt more at ease, where you felt comfortable and connected to tradition and nature. A room that embraced you with its serene energy, a sanctuary from the noise and chaos of the modern world.

Japandi isn't just an aesthetic; it's an invitation to slow down, to breathe deeply, and to reconnect with the natural world around us. It's a rebellion against the cluttered and overstimulated, a conscious choice to embrace minimalism and intentionality in our living spaces.

Over the following pages, we'll explore the art of Japandi, a timeless blend of two cultures united by their reverence for craftsmanship, functionality, and a deep respect for nature's beauty. We'll uncover the principles that guide this design philosophy, the colors that breathe life into these spaces, and the textures that invite us to touch and feel the world around us.

But more than that, we'll discover the power of intentional living, of creating environments that nurture our souls and remind us of what truly matters. Because in a world that often demands our attention and energy, Japandi offers a sanctuary, a place to pause and reconnect with the essence of what it means to be human.

So, join me on this journey, and let's explore the art of Japandi style.

Minimalistic Japanese apartment living space

Scandinavian loft living space

Japandi theme apartment living room

Chapter 1: Introduction to Japandi Style

Welcome to the world of Japandi, a harmonious fusion of Japanese aesthetics and Scandinavian design principles. In this book, we will discover the essence of Japandi style, exploring its origins, core principles, and practical applications in creating beautiful, functional, and serene living spaces.

But before we go anywhere, let's start by defining what Japandi style stands for. As a fusion of East and West, Japandi represents the convergence of Japanese aesthetics with Scandinavian design principles. This unique blend combines the timeless elegance and minimalism of Japanese design with the functionality and warmth of Scandinavian interiors. The result is a style that embodies simplicity, serenity, and a deep appreciation for craftsmanship and natural elements.

In recent times, Japandi style has gained worldwide popularity for its ability to create spaces that are both visually striking and emotionally soothing. By combining the warmth and texture of Scandinavian design with the serenity and mindfulness of Japanese aesthetics, Japandi offers a refreshing and rejuvenating approach to interior design that resonates with modern homeowners seeking a sanctuary of calm amidst the chaos of everyday life.

Japandi style has quickly gained widespread recognition in the design world too, with influential designers and brands embracing its principles. From furniture collections inspired by traditional Japanese craftsmanship to Scandinavian-inspired accessories, the market is filled with products that reflect the ethos of Japandi design principles.

In this book, we will delve into the key elements of Japandi style, from its emphasis on simplicity and functionality to its use of natural materials and clean lines. We will explore how Japandi style can be applied in different rooms of the house, from the living room to the bedroom to the kitchen and beyond, with practical tips and real-life examples to inspire and guide you along the way.

Origins & Evolution

Before delving deeper into the world of Japandi style and design, it's essential to understand its origins and evolution. By appreciating the cultural heritage and design philosophies that have shaped this aesthetic, you can gain a better understanding of its principles and how to incorporate them into your own living space.

First, the evolution of Japandi style has been mixed and influenced by various factors, including globalization, urbanization, and the rise of social media. Second, while the term has come to prominence in recent years, the cross-pollination of design principles has its roots in the early decades of exchange between Japan and the Scandinavian countries of Denmark, Sweden, and Norway over 150 years ago.

Following the 1854 Treaty of Kanagawa—which allowed Western nations to trade with Japan after 220 years of self-enforced isolation—designers, architects, and other creatives from Europe ventured to Japan for the very first time.

One of the influential figures during this time was the Danish naval lieutenant William Carstensen, who, in the 1860s, journeyed to Tokyo (formerly known as "Edo") to immerse himself in Japanese culture. His experiences, detailed in his publication "Japan's Capital and the Japanese," sparked early interest in Japanese lifestyle, crafts, and design principles within his native home of Denmark.

However, cultural exchange between Japan and Europe over the following 90 years remained constricted by two major world wars, vast distances of land and ocean, and slow physical communication channels.

These constraints began to ease in the middle of the 20th Century, during a period of accelerated cultural exchange and appreciation between Japan and Scandinavia. The post-war era also marked a shift towards a more interconnected world, with advancements in technology and transportation facilitating the exchange of ideas, goods, and culture at an unprecedented scale.

In both Japan and Scandinavia, there were significant social and economic transformations at play, leading to a reevaluation of traditional design principles. In Japan, the post-World War II era oversaw a shift towards simplicity and functionality in design. Influenced by concepts such as Zen Buddhism and the tea ceremony, Japanese designers sought to create spaces that promoted tranquility and mindfulness. Minimalism served as a guiding principle, emphasizing the beauty of clean lines, uncluttered spaces, and the use of natural materials.

In Scandinavia, the post-war period oversaw the embrace of minimalism as well, but with a distinct focus on functionality, social equality, and accessibility in design. The region's designers championed the idea of "democratic design", aiming to produce affordable, high-quality items that could enhance the everyday lives of many and not just a few. This ethos was rooted in the broader social welfare principles prevalent in Scandinavian countries emphasizing inclusivity and the well-being of the community.

Equally, designers were keen to explore ways to combine aesthetics with emotional functionality. The concept of "hygge" in Denmark and "lagom" in Sweden emphasized the importance of creating cozy, balanced environments that could foster a sense of well-being, for example.

During this same period, the ongoing development of Japanese and Scandinavian design philosophies fostered mutual admiration and influence among Japanese and Scandinavian designers. The shared values of simplicity, functionality, and a profound respect for nature and materials facilitated an advance in the exchange of ideas and inspirations. Exhibitions, design symposiums, and academic exchanges became platforms for dialogue, further strengthening the ties between the two regions.

The second half of the 20th Century saw the rise of iconic designers and architects from both regions, whose works epitomized the shared values in design principles. Figures such as Verner Panton and Arne Jacobsen from Scandinavia, and Isamu Noguchi and Kenzo Tange from Japan became influential not only in their respective regions but also on the global stage, further disseminating the principles of their cultural design ethos.

The influence of their design principles was commercialized and popularized by companies like IKEA, which played a pivotal role in spreading Scandinavian design to a global audience. Similarly, Japanese design concepts found their way into international markets, influencing product design, architecture, and interior decorating trends globally.

The legacy of the post-war era and its accelerated globalization ultimately culminated in a convergence of these two design traditions, giving rise to what we now call Japandi style. This distinct style was pioneered by a collection of designers including Niels Gammelgaard from Denmark in the late 20th Century. Influenced by Japanese wabi-sabi philosophy and Danish modernism, Gammelgaard fused these two aesthetics into what he dubbed "the feeling of Japan and the thinking of Scandinavia." Embodying the best of both concepts, this new design trend captured the shared values of simplicity, functionality, and a profound connection to nature.

In terms of aesthetics, Gammelgaard's work married the minimalism and craftsmanship of Japanese design with the warmth and comfort of Scandinavian interiors. The result was a harmonious blend of clean lines, neutral color palettes, and natural textures that evoked a sense of calm and serenity.

This original rendering of Japandi gained initial followers in Europe during the 1990s, especially among Scandinavian designers integrating Japanese influences. By the early 2000s, Japandi proponents started to appear in North America and other countries outside of Scandinavia.

As the "mid-century modern style" evolved in the 2010s, Japandi's clean-lined and natural look developed into a popular update for modern households. This trend was supported by lifestyle bloggers and sites like *The Spruce*, Amsterdam-based *Modest Minimalist* blog, and Ariene Hong's *Iconic Life* blog, which helped to showcase Japandi style as an elegant solution to modern design priorities including sustainability, multifunctionality, and creating a seamless blend between indoor and outdoor spaces.

Today Japandi continues to break into the mainstream through social media and e-commerce websites like Instagram, Pinterest, and Etsy. Notable influencers include Justina Blakeney and her Jungalow brand promoting the "boho Japandi" style with a

Bohemian touch. Meanwhile, stores like Anthropologie and Article, feature Japandi collections for wider audiences.

While Japandi style has gained popularity in various countries around the world, the style remains most appreciated in Japan and Scandinavian countries, due to close exposure and the alignment of cultural aesthetics and design principles. That said, Japandi style has seen a surge in interest in other countries including the United States, the United Kingdom, Singapore, Poland, Australia, and the Netherlands. This recent rise in global popularity has been significantly bolstered by virality-based social apps like Instagram and TikTok, where the style's harmonious and aesthetically pleasing visuals resonate with the current trend towards a more mindful and slower-paced lifestyle.

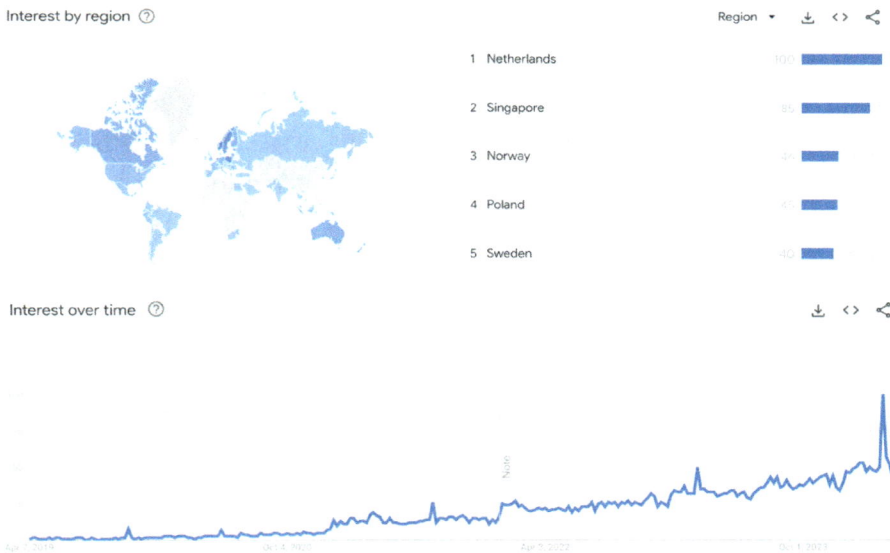

Google Trends data for the search term "Japandi"

Types of homeowners

When it comes to demographics, Japandi works well for homeowners of all ages and has broad appeal across a spectrum of people and lifestyles, including minimalists, nature lovers, and quality-conscious shoppers, as discussed in this section.

Minimalists: Japandi's integration of minimalist principles including sustainability and eco-friendliness fits well with minimalists. They are also attracted to Japandi's use of natural materials and long-lasting quality.

Cultural enthusiasts: Japandi's unique blend of distinct cultural aesthetics appeals to people fascinated by cultural fusion and the integration of different design philosophies.

Comfort seekers: Consumers who value comfort and a cozy atmosphere in their homes may be drawn by the Scandinavian influence and the concept of hygge, which emphasizes comfort and warmth alongside minimalist design.

Nature lowers: The integration of natural elements such as wood, bamboo, and plants makes Japandi appealing to those who enjoy bringing the outdoors into their homes and fostering a closer connection with nature.

Quality-conscious shoppers: Japandi's emphasis on fine craftsmanship and high-quality materials resonates with consumers willing to invest in durable and well-made furniture and décor. Japandi's focus on craftsmanship and artisanal products also supports sustainable living practices.

Trend followers: As long as Japandi is new and chic, it will attract people who want to keep up with the latest trends in interior design and who want to incorporate contemporary aesthetics into their homes.

Business owners: Japandi style may be suitable for small business owners looking to create a stylish and sustainable decor, especially as it creates a serene and inviting atmosphere for customers.

Urban dwellers: With minimalism and functionality well-suited for city living, Japandi is an easy way to create a stylish and functional space in a small urban space.

Japandi vs. MUJI

Although Japandi and MUJI share similarities, they are not the same style. Japandi style represents a fusion of Japanese and Scandinavian design principles, whereas MUJI refers to a

Japanese retail company that embodies the ideals of minimalism, functionality, and simplicity in its brand and product design. In Japanese, the name MUJI means "no brand, quality goods" with the word "mu" meaning "nothing" or "empty" and "ji" meaning "thing" or "article."

The popular retail store was founded in 1980 by the Seiyu Japanese supermarket chain with a mission to offer generic, unbranded versions of products sold in other stores. At the time, the founder of the brand, Ikko Tanaka, wanted to challenge excessive branding, packaging, and other design norms popular during the 1970s.

MUJI's initial offerings, centered on stationery and storage solutions, embodied the essence of functionality and simplicity over branding. Over time, the brand broadened its selection to include apparel, furniture, household items, food, and beyond, while still showcasing its commitment to simplicity and functionality across a more diverse product range.

Thus, while MUJI and Japandi style share a common preference for minimalism, utility, and wellness, the MUJI store is not a full reflection of Japandi style. For one, Japandi style distinctly incorporates Scandinavian preferences for metal and stone, which contrasts with MUJI's predominant use of wood and fabric in its products.

Second, Japandi emphasizes artisanal customization and personal expression through handicrafts and architecture tailored to individual needs, which differs from MUJI's more standardized approach to home decor. Japandi spaces are also enriched with plants and greenery, seamlessly blending indoor and outdoor environments with lush greenery, while MUJI trends to promote large, open areas left intentionally unoccupied or minimally furnished, creating a sense of simplicity and spaciousness in the home.

Despite these differences, you will observe similarities between MUJI and Japandi, such as a neutral color palette, the embrace of natural materials like wood, cotton, wool, and linen, clean lines and shapes, and a constant emphasis on multifunctionality. So, while MUJI does offer a glimpse into Japandi aesthetics, you will need to venture outside the popular retail store to find the true essence of Japandi style.

Japandi vs. Minimalism

Another common question centers around the line between Japandi and Minimalism design, prompting questions about what makes these two styles unique and distinct.

While both styles prioritize quality over quantity, Minimalism and Japandi differ in their goals and implementation. Minimalism embraces simplicity and impersonality, eliminating ornaments, objects, and distractions. In contrast, Japandi removes clutter and embraces clean lines to create airy, harmonious spaces that promote connection with one's environment.

Another primary distinction between Japandi and Minimalism lies in their approach to warmth. Japandi weaves in more textures and elements of nature, offering a cozier feel, whereas Minimalism often presents a cooler, more austere appearance.

Consequently, Japandi style appeals more to those desiring a serene and welcoming atmosphere enriched with natural textures and an elegant Japanese-Scandinavian influence. Minimalism, meanwhile, is ideal for those seeking a space defined purely by simplicity.

That said, blending elements from both styles might be the answer to your unique minimalist haven. For instance, integrating Japandi's rich textures into a minimalist setting or infusing warmth into a space with subtle color accents are two ways to harmonize these aesthetics, creating a living space that is unique and reflective of personal taste.

Japandi vs. Wabi-sabi

While Japandi and wabi-sabi promote a connection with nature, they also remain two distinct styles. The main difference between Japandi and wabi-sabi is their aesthetic approach. Japandi fuses minimalism, clean lines, and functionality while wabi-sabi embraces natural imperfection.

Furniture and décor in Japandi style will often feature simple yet elegant designs with a focus on practicality and space optimization. Conversely, wabi-sabi embraces the beauty of imperfection, impermanence, and simplicity. Valuing authenticity and the passage of time, it finds beauty in the natural, the weathered, and the irregular. In wabi-sabi design, you'll often find handmade or artisanal pieces, organic materials, and a sense of rustic charm. Also, while Japandi strives for a harmonious balance between simplicity and functionality, wabi-sabi celebrates the beauty found in the flaws and imperfections of everyday objects and materials. This distinction in aesthetic approach leads to different design outcomes and atmospheres in living spaces, with Japandi evoking a more polished, minimalistic, and modern feel, whereas wabi-sabi fosters appreciation for life's imperfection and the beauty of age.

What is NOT Japandi Style

To fully understand and embrace the unique characteristics of the Japandi style, it's valuable to highlight scenarios that deviate from this aesthetic.

1. A cluttered space with excessive furniture pieces and ornaments.
2. An atmosphere that is dark and heavy, saturated with dark wood and excessive earthy tones.
3. A purely Scandinavian space lacking Japanese elements and cultural references, or vice versa.
4. A simple space focused purely on functionality and minimalism with no reference to comfort or coziness.

Chapter 2: Japanese & Scandinavian Influences

Exploring Japanese Aesthetics

In Japan, traditional aesthetics are deeply rooted in the country's rich cultural and philosophical history, spanning centuries of artistic expression and craftsmanship. By studying Japanese aesthetics, you can gain useful insights into a design tradition that values harmony, balance, and a deep connection to nature. Rooms, for example, are often designed to flow seamlessly from one to the next, blurring the boundaries between separate rooms. Lighting, meanwhile, is typically gentle, creating a soothing and peaceful ambiance using paper-covered lamps or ceramic lanterns.

In relation to design, minimalism is one of the guiding principles, emphasizing the importance of stripping away the unnecessary to reveal the essence of a form or space with furnishings and decorations kept to a minimum. Less is more when it comes to Japandi and items or designs shouldn't need to compete against each other for attention. This minimalist approach can be seen in traditional Japanese architecture, where clean lines, open spaces, and the use of carefully chosen materials create a sense of tranquility and harmony.

Another aspect of Japanese aesthetics is the use of natural materials, such as wood, paper, and bamboo. Throughout history, Japanese craftsmen and craftswomen have employed traditional techniques such as joinery and weaving to create objects that are both functional and aesthetically pleasing, reflecting a deep respect for natural materials and the processes used to transform them. Walls, for example, often employ soft, earthen colors, paper screens as well as bamboo or wooden finishes. These materials are valued not only for their beauty but also for their connection to nature. Japanese interiors also incorporate ample greenery, fostering a harmonious connection with nature.

In addition to minimalism and natural materials, Japanese aesthetics are characterized by a keen attention to detail and a sense of mindfulness in everyday life. From the arrangement of objects in a room to the rituals of tea ceremonies and flower arranging, Japanese culture places great importance on the beauty of small gestures and the appreciation of fleeting moments.

To appreciate Japanese aesthetics at a deeper level, we will now unpack the three principles of wabi-sabi, shibui, and yūgen.

Wabi-sabi

As one of the central concepts in Japanese aesthetics, wabi-sabi celebrates the beauty of imperfection, impermanence, and the natural world. The concept originated in China but evolved seven hundred years ago into a Japanese ideal with strong links to Zen Buddhism. Traditionally, it was honored by the Japanese nobility as a reaction against heavy ornamentation and lavishness. Now, in modern times, wabi-sabi represents the embrace of beauty in imperfection and being at peace with the imperfections of the modern world. As discussed in the previous chapter, wabi-sabi embraces the natural cycle of growth and decay, celebrating the flaws and quirks that come with handmade objects and the natural world.

In Japandi interiors, the influence of wabi-sabi is found in the choice of natural materials such as untreated wood, stone, and ceramics. Unlike artificial materials, which may deteriorate or show signs of wear in a less appealing manner, natural materials tend to retain their aesthetic appeal even as they age. They age with grace, developing a patina and character that adds to their beauty and charm. An example of this is hardwood floors, which tend to develop a rich, warm hue over time, while leather upholstery may acquire a soft, supple texture with use. These natural aging processes not only enhance the visual appeal of the materials but also contribute to a sense of authenticity and timelessness in interior spaces.

Another example of wabi-sabi is the kintsugi technique, which translates to "golden joinery" in Japanese. This is a centuries-old art form and philosophy, which involves repairing broken pottery with lacquer dusted or mixed with powdered gold, silver, or platinum. The practice emerged in an era when resources were less abundant, and it was common to repair household items rather than replace them.

Practically speaking, Kintsugi not only restores the functionality of the ceramic piece but transforms it into a unique work of art, highlighting the cracks and repairs as part of the object's history rather than something to disguise.

The following photo showcases a traditional Japanese teapot (designed for brewing green tea) alongside two mugs repaired using the kintsugi technique.

Shibui

The next aesthetic principle, shibui (pronounced "see-boo-ee") values elegant simplicity and subtle or austere beauty. The term itself translates to "astringent" or "bitter" but takes on a more positive connotation when describing aesthetics and design topics in the Japanese language.

As part of its core principles, shibui celebrates simplicity, emptiness, and everyday functionality while finding beauty in natural raw materials rather than ornamentation. Additionally, it focuses on pure, quiet forms stripped down to their essence, which take the form of the following traits:

1. Clean lines, negative space, natural materials
2. A subtle and earthy color palette
3. Handcrafted items with an acceptance of natural flaws
4. Minimalism and tranquility

You will notice aspects of shibui in wabi-sabi philosophy and the embrace of imperfection. Shibui also interlinks with MUJI and its core principles of essential and minimalistic design.

Yūgen

Yūgen, meaning "subtle and profound grace," is another important concept in traditional Japanese aesthetics. The term comes from the Chinese word "youan," meaning dark and obscure, and was first adopted in Japan by monks as a way to describe spiritual enlightenment. In design circles, the term refers to an appreciation for beauty that is felt rather than overtly seen, focusing on what is hidden while leaving space for the imagination.

In the case of art, an example of yūgen might be a calligraphic work or traditional Japanese painting that captures the essence of a subject through minimal brushstrokes, leaving room for interpretation and contemplation. In architecture, it might manifest in the graceful curves designed to harmonize with the natural surroundings and evoke a sense of tranquility and depth.

The concept of yūgen also aligns with the Japandi design philosophy, which seeks to create harmonious and serene living spaces that foster a connection with nature, introspection, and a sense of tranquility. In addition, both aesthetics value simplicity, subtlety, and the use of negative space to evoke a sense of calm, balance, and contemplation.

Unpacking Scandinavian Design Concepts

Rooted in the design heritage of Denmark, Sweden, and Norway, Scandinavian or Scandi style is a harmonious blend of functionality and aesthetics. This iconic aesthetic spread in the early 20th Century during the golden age of Scandinavian design, when visionary European designers like Arne Jacobsen (Denmark), Verner Panton (Denmark), Josef Frank (Austrian), and Alvar Aalto (Finland) pioneered a minimalist yet beautiful approach to interiors and furnishings.

At its core, Scandinavian design is characterized by a clean and pared-down aesthetic that seeks to combine practicality with visual appeal. The style shuns excessive ornamentation and clutter, instead celebrating the essence of each product or space. Furnishings and decorations are kept to a minimum, creating a sense of calm and tranquility that permeates the atmosphere.

Lighting plays a crucial role in Scandinavian interiors, as these countries experience limited natural light during the long winter months. Designers have therefore mastered the art of incorporating lighting in innovative ways, creating bright and airy spaces that combat the darkness outside.

Another major hallmark of Scandinavian design is the focus on natural materials and craftsmanship. From the sleek lines of teak furniture to the tactile warmth of woven textiles, Scandinavian designers have a deep appreciation for the beauty of wood, leather, and other natural materials. Natural materials such as cotton, wool, linen, and wood are prominently featured, lending a warmth and organic quality. House plants are often incorporated, adding a touch of greenery and further reinforcing the connection between indoor and outdoor environments. Craftsmanship is highly valued in Scandinavian culture too, with designers collaborating closely with skilled artisans to create pieces that are both functional and aesthetically pleasing.

In addition to natural materials and craftsmanship, Scandinavian design is characterized by its commitment to functionality and simplicity. Every element within a space is thoughtfully chosen for its practicality and utility, with an emphasis on clean lines and uncluttered spaces. This means that Scandinavian interiors are mostly free of unnecessary ornamentation, allowing the beauty of the materials and the design itself to take center stage.

Scandinavian design is also rooted in cultural influences that extend beyond aesthetics, including the values of equality, social responsibility, and democratic design, which profoundly inform design decisions and practices.

Equality is a fundamental pillar of Scandinavian society, and this ethos permeates into design philosophy. Typically, Scandinavian designers strive to create inclusive spaces and products accessible to all, regardless of socioeconomic status or background. This commitment to equality is reflected in the democratization of design, where emphasis is often placed on affordability and functionality without sacrificing quality or style. Designs are crafted with the intention of enhancing the lives of everyone and contributing to a more equitable and inclusive society.

Likewise, social responsibility is another cornerstone of Scandinavian design, driven by a collective consciousness to address pressing societal and environmental challenges. Designers prioritize sustainable practices, opting for eco-friendly materials and production methods to minimize environmental impact. By adopting a holistic approach to sustainability, Scandinavian design seeks to mitigate resource depletion, reduce waste, and promote ecological stewardship. This includes a strong emphasis on ethical labor practices, with designers advocating for fair wages, safe working conditions, and ethical sourcing throughout the supply chain.

Democratic design principles underscore the belief that good design should be accessible, functional, and aesthetically pleasing to the masses. Scandinavian designers therefore embrace simplicity and practicality, focusing on creating products that serve a genuine need and enhance everyday life. This approach contrasts with elitist notions of design, prioritizing utility over ornamentation and elitism. By democratizing design, Scandinavian designers empower individuals to make informed choices and express their own personal style, fostering a sense of ownership and empowerment within communities.

Scandinavian design also reflects a commitment to social cohesion and collective well-being. Whether it be communal gathering spaces, shared public amenities, or inclusive design practices, Scandinavian designers prioritize the collective good over individual interests, fostering a sense of solidarity and cohesion within society. Spaces are therefore designed to promote interaction, collaboration, and a sense of belonging, fostering social connections and community engagement.

Hygge

Over the past decade, Scandinavia, and specifically, Denmark, have become well-known globally for the lifestyle and design principles of hygge. As one of the key principles of Danish design, "hygge" is a Danish term that embodies a feeling of coziness, contentment, and well-being.

In Sweden, a similar concept to "hygge" is "mysig," which also refers to a cozy and comfortable atmosphere. In Norway, they have a term called "koselig," which shares similar sentiments of warmth, comfort, and intimacy. These concepts are all deeply rooted in Scandinavian culture and reflect a shared appreciation for creating inviting and nurturing environments.

Each of these design concepts is characterized by soft lighting, comfortable furnishings, and warm, inviting textures that create a sense of sanctuary in the home. This emphasis on comfort and relaxation is central to Scandinavian design philosophy, reflecting the region's long, dark winters and the importance of creating spaces that provide refuge from the elements.

Whether it's sharing a home-cooked meal with loved ones, hosting a game night with friends, or simply enjoying a quiet moment of companionship with a partner or pet, hygge is also about nurturing relationships and creating moments of togetherness and meaningful connections with others.

In practice, hygge can be achieved through soft lighting, plush textiles, and comfortable furnishings that encourage relaxation and intimacy. Candles are another quintessential hygge accessory, adding warmth and ambiance to any space and creating a sense of hygge even on the darkest of winter nights. In fact, according to *The Little Book of Hygge*, 28% of people in Denmark light candles daily.

In addition to creating a cozy and inviting home environment, hygge emphasizes the importance of self-care and well-being. This can include practices such as mindfulness, meditation, and self-reflection, as well as indulging in activities that bring joy and fulfillment such as taking a long bath, going for a leisurely walk in nature, or practicing a creative hobby.

Tea Culture

Tea and coffee hold significant cultural significance in Japan and Scandinavia, transcending their roles as mere beverages and serving as expressions of lifestyle and a cherished tradition that can bring people together.

In Japan, the tea ceremony, known as chanoyu (literally "hot water for tea"), is an intricate ritual steeped in centuries of tradition and philosophy. The ceremony revolves around the preparation and serving of matcha, a finely ground green tea, accompanied by traditional Japanese sweets. The tea ceremony is a meticulously choreographed experience that offers a respite from the stresses of everyday life by immersing participants in the Zen aesthetics of serenity and peace.

In Scandinavia, the tradition of fika holds a similarly revered place in the cultural fabric. Originating in Sweden, fika is much more than a regular coffee break; it is a conscious act of slowing down and savoring the moment. Fika involves taking a deliberate pause from one's activities to enjoy a cup of coffee or tea, often accompanied by a sweet treat, in the company of friends, family, or colleagues.

Importantly, Fika is a therapeutic practice that promotes well-being and productivity by encouraging individuals to step back from the hustle and bustle of daily life and engage in genuine relaxation and social connection. It is a cherished ritual that fosters a sense of community, allowing people to come together and share in the simple pleasures of good company and conversation over a warm beverage.

These deeply ingrained cultural practices in both regions demonstrate the profound impact that a simple act, such as sharing a cup of tea or coffee, can have on individual and societal well-being. They serve as reminders to embrace the present, appreciate the beauty in the ordinary, and cherish the moments that bring people together in a shared experience of comfort and connection.

Chapter 3: Essential Elements of Japandi Style

Minimalism: Less is More

At the core of Japandi style lies the principle of minimalism, an aesthetic philosophy that celebrates simplicity, functionality, and the elimination of excess. Rooted in both Japanese and Scandinavian design traditions, minimalism emphasizes the importance of stripping away unnecessary ornamentation to reveal the essence of a form or space. Minimalism, therefore, is not about deprivation or austerity; rather, it's about prioritizing quality over quantity and creating spaces that are both beautiful and functional.

One of the key benefits of minimalism is its ability to promote a sense of calm and clarity in the home. By removing excess clutter and simplifying the environment, minimalism creates a peaceful retreat from the chaos of modern life. This sense of tranquility not only enhances physical well-being but also allows people to focus their attention on the things that truly matter.

In addition to promoting a sense of calm, minimalism encourages people to be more mindful and intentional in their consumption habits. By adopting a less-is-more mentality, people can learn to appreciate the beauty of simplicity and cultivate a deeper connection to the objects and spaces in their lives. Instead of accumulating possessions for the sake of it, they can focus on acquiring items that bring them joy and serve a purpose.

In Japandi interiors, minimalism is evident in every aspect of the design, from the architecture and furniture to the décor and accessories. Spaces are carefully curated to create a sense of openness and tranquility, with clean lines, uncluttered surfaces, and a focus on negative space. By reducing visual noise and unnecessary distractions, minimalism allows the beauty of the materials and the design to shine through.

Lastly, minimalism is often complemented by natural materials, muted color palettes, and thoughtful design details that add warmth and character to the space.

Wood, Stone & Textiles

In Japandi design, the use of natural materials extends beyond aesthetics to reflect a deeper connection to the environment and a respect for the natural world. By incorporating materials that are sustainable, renewable, and locally sourced, designers can create spaces that are not only beautiful but also environmentally conscious. This commitment to sustainability aligns with the principles of Japanese and Scandinavian design, which prioritize harmony with nature and the responsible usage of resources.

Likewise, by embracing natural materials in their various forms, Japandi interiors achieve a sense of timelessness and authenticity that resonates with people of all backgrounds. Whether it's the warmth of wood, the solidity of stone, or the softness of textiles, these materials contribute to a sense of balance and well-being in the home.

Wood, in particular, plays a prominent role in Japandi interiors, especially as it is hard-wearing and easy to maintain. From furniture and flooring to architectural details and tableware, wood is utilized in a variety of ways to create a sense of warmth and authenticity with its warm tones and rich textures. Some unique examples include slatted walls to create visual interest, posters or photos housed in wooden frames, and wooden coffee tables with thick knots visible on their surface.

When it comes to cultivating a more Scandinavian feel to your home, try to look for dark shades of wood such as walnut or mahogany. For a Japanese-inspired atmosphere, consider incorporating bamboo or lighter shades of wood such as ash and maple. The former can be used for flooring, accessories, other furnishings, or simply as a living tree. Bamboo is also a biodegradable and renewable resource that regenerates quickly after harvesting, making it a smart, sustainable option.

In addition to wood, Japandi style embraces other natural materials like stone, bamboo, paper, and rattan. Stone, with its cool tones and tactile qualities, adds a sense of solidity and permanence to the space, and is often used in bathrooms and kitchens, including limestone, marble, and terrasso. Bamboo and rattan, meanwhile, bring a touch of natural elegance and texture to furniture and décor accents.

When it comes to paper, you will often see the use of traditional Japanese paper made from natural fibers like mulberry, hemp, or rice straw, which are more durable than traditional forms of paper. Known as washi paper, Japanese paper is renowned for its lightweight and delicate texture, making it an ideal material for many applications in interior design. Its translucent quality allows diffused light to filter through, creating a soft and inviting ambiance reminiscent of traditional Japanese interiors. You will see washi paper used for shoji screens, window treatments, lampshades, umbrellas, lanterns, sliding doors, and decorative panels.

Textiles are another essential element of Japandi style, adding softness, warmth, and visual interest to the space. From simple linen curtains to cozy wool throws, drapery, upholstery, and cushions, these textiles play a key role in creating a sense of coziness and comfort in Japandi interiors. Natural fibers such as cotton, linen, and wool are preferred for their comfort and breathability, as well as their eco-friendliness and ability to age gracefully over time. Switching out fabric items like rugs and floor cushions is also a fun method to refresh your home with the changing seasons. This could involve using linen-covered pieces in the summer for a light and airy feel, while choosing woolen items for added warmth and coziness during the colder winter months.

Finding Harmony Underfoot

Covering a large surface area, flooring can have a major influence on the visual perspective, look, and feel of an area. In the quest to create a Japandi-inspired sanctuary, the choice of flooring is vitally important. Whether its opting for the timeless beauty of wood, the sustainable softness of cork, the modern simplicity of concrete, the natural grace of bamboo, or the versatile elegance of vinyl, each option has the potential to deliver a positive underfoot experience.

Wood flooring is typically a cornerstone of Japandi style, embodying the warmth, texture, and organic charm that define this aesthetic. From the light, airy hues of oak to the rich, earthy tones of walnut, wood flooring brings a sense of serenity and connection to nature to any room.

For those who prioritize sustainability without compromising on comfort, cork flooring is also an excellent choice. Harvested from the bark of cork oak trees, cork flooring is not only eco-friendly but also offers a soft, cushioned feel underfoot. Its natural acoustic properties make it an ideal option for creating quiet, tranquil environments reminiscent of traditional Japanese interiors.

Bamboo flooring is another popular choice, thanks to its natural beauty, sustainability, and durability. As one of the fastest-growing plants on earth, bamboo is an eco-friendly alternative to traditional hardwoods. Its subtle grain patterns and warm, honey-toned hues bring a sense of natural grace and serenity to any room, while its exceptional durability makes it well-suited for busy households. Whether installed as planks or tiles, bamboo flooring adds a touch of organic elegance to Japandi interiors.

For a more contemporary take on Japandi design, concrete flooring offers a sleek, minimalist aesthetic that exudes modern sophistication. Whether polished to a smooth finish or left raw for an industrial edge, concrete flooring provides a versatile canvas for expressing the clean lines and geometric shapes characteristic of Scandinavian and Japanese design. Its durability and low-maintenance nature make it a practical choice for high-traffic areas, while its cool, understated elegance adds a touch of urban chic to any space. That said, you will sacrifice some of the warmth and the connection with nature that is felt with wooden floors.

Next, for those seeking a practical yet stylish flooring option for their space, vinyl flooring offers an interesting alternative. Available in a wide range of colors, patterns, and textures, vinyl flooring offers versatility and durability without compromising on aesthetics. Its water-resistant properties make it ideal for kitchens and bathrooms, while its affordability and low-maintenance nature make it a practical choice for modern living. Whether opting for luxury vinyl plank (LVP) or luxury vinyl tile (LVT), you can achieve the look and feel of natural materials without the upkeep.

As highlighted, when it comes to flooring options for Japandi-inspired spaces, there's no shortage of choices. Whether you prefer the natural warmth of wood, the eco-friendly appeal of cork, the modern simplicity of concrete, the organic elegance of bamboo, or the versatile practicality of vinyl, there's a flooring option to suit every taste and lifestyle. Ultimately, the key is to choose a flooring material that not only complements the aesthetic of your space but also fits your budget and personal preferences.

Clean Lines

Clean lines and functional design are fundamental aspects of Japandi style,
contributing to a sense of simplicity and elegance. You will see this in the choice of furniture and architectural elements, which often feature straight, angular shapes that create a sense of order and balance. By eliminating unnecessary ornamentation and decorative flourishes, clean lines allow the beauty of the materials and the design to come through.

Example of a couch with clean lines vs. a couch with intricate lines

Above is a side-by-side comparison showcasing the contrast between a Scandi-style couch with clean lines and a more traditional and decorative couch without clean lines. This visual emphasizes the differences in design philosophy, from simplicity and functionality to ornate details and curves.

Art: Finding Zen in Spaces

Art plays a special role in adding a personal touch and elevating the ambiance of a room or space, and in the context of the Japandi style, it also serves as a crucial element in achieving harmony and balance. While art is inherently subjective, there are several key considerations to keep in mind when selecting pieces that complement the essence of Japandi design.

First and foremost, Japandi embraces natural materials and a tranquil color scheme, mirroring the calm and organic elements of nature. When choosing art, it's advisable to choose minimalist or monochrome pieces that integrate with your decor's color palette. Art that juxtaposes neutral tones such as white, grey, and beige with darker hues like brown, traditional Japanese reds, or deep blacks can create striking visual contrasts that enhance the overall aesthetic. Additionally, subtle pops of pale pink or sky blue can inject a sense of serenity and warmth into the space, paying homage to the Scandi influence on Japandi style.

Next, you may want to incorporate artwork that adds texture and depth to the space, mirroring the tactile qualities of other elements within the room. This might mean choosing artwork that has natural textures such as woodcut prints, woven textiles, or handcrafted ceramics. These tactile elements can enhance the sensory experience and create visual interest within the space.

Similarly, you might want to explore artwork that celebrates nature and the natural world such as botanical prints, landscape paintings, or abstract representations of natural forms. These nature-inspired motifs can evoke a sense of serenity and connection to the outdoors.

In keeping with the principles of Japandi design, you may want to pursue balance and symmetry when arranging your artwork. This can be achieved by pairing larger pieces with smaller ones or by arranging multiple pieces in a balanced manner. Symmetrical arrangements can also help establish a sense of order and tranquility within the space.

Another crucial aspect to consider is the size of the artwork. In Japandi interiors, large statement pieces are often used to create focal points and anchor the room's aesthetic. Before selecting a size, take stock of the room's furniture arrangement and assess the ceiling height. High ceilings can accommodate larger artworks, while lower ceilings may benefit from lower canvas heights or landscape-oriented pieces that visually elongate the space.

Additionally, consider the viewing distance when determining the appropriate size of the artwork. To fully appreciate a piece, you want to be able to view it from a certain distance. As a general rule of thumb, you should multiply the diagonal measurement of the artwork by 1.5 to determine the optimal viewing distance. In spaces with limited square footage, such as narrow hallways or staircases, you should opt for smaller pieces of art that complement the scale of the area. These smaller artworks can still make a significant impact while ensuring that the space feels balanced and uncluttered.

Finally, it is valuable to pay attention to lighting when displaying artwork, as proper illumination can significantly impact its appearance and impact within the space. Consider installing adjustable spotlights or wall-mounted fixtures to highlight focal points and create a gallery-like ambiance. Also, avoid placing artwork in direct sunlight, as prolonged exposure can cause fading or damage to delicate materials.

Above all, don't be afraid to experiment and have fun with your art selections. Japandi design encourages a sense of creativity and individual expression, so feel free to mix and match different styles, colors, and mediums until you find the combination that reflects your unique aesthetic preference.

Harmony & Balance: Finding Zen in Spaces

Harmony and balance are central tenets of Japandi style, reflecting the influence of Japanese Zen philosophy and Scandinavian design principles.

Symmetry and proportion are two of the key ways in which harmony and balance are achieved in Japandi interiors. Spaces are carefully balanced with furniture and accessories arranged in a way that feels both cohesive and inviting. Symmetrical arrangements help to create a sense of order and stability, while carefully proportioned elements contribute to a feeling of balance and proportionality.

In addition to symmetry and proportion, harmony and balance in Japandi style can be achieved through the use of complementary colors and materials. Neutral color palettes dominated by shades of beige, gray, and taupe create a sense of unity and cohesion throughout the space, while accents of black or dark wood add depth and contrast.

In Japandi interiors, the concept of "ma," or negative space, is also important in creating a sense of balance and harmony. Empty spaces are valued as much as filled ones, allowing for moments of pause and reflection in the home. By embracing the beauty of emptiness and allowing space to breathe, Japandi interiors achieve a sense of tranquility and balance that is essential to their aesthetic.

Another key aspect of harmony and balance in Japandi style is the incorporation of elements that evoke a sense of calm and tranquility. From soft lighting and natural textures to minimalist décor and uncluttered spaces, every detail is chosen to create a serene and inviting atmosphere. By eliminating distractions and creating a sense of simplicity, Japandi interiors encourage mindfulness and relaxation, allowing you to feel grounded and centered in your surroundings.

Chapter 4: Color Palette & Textures

One of the hallmarks of Japandi style is its unique color palette. Whereas Scandinavian interiors often feature crisp whites, off-whites, and pops of gentle hues like blues, greens, and pastels, Japanese interiors tend to draw inspiration from nature, showcasing deeper tones such as rich browns, deep greens, and warm taupes.

As a result, the Japandi color palette aims to strike a delicate balance between these two contrasting approaches. It combines the light and airy Scandinavian color scheme with the earthy, grounding tones characteristic of Japanese design.

Over the following pages, we will explore a variety of different Japandi color options including neutral hues and accent colors before discussing popular textures that you can use in your own home.

Neutral Hues: Embracing Simplicity

Neutral hues form the cornerstone of the Japandi color palette, reflecting the minimalist principles of design traditions in both regions. Embracing simplicity and understatement, neutral colors create a serene and timeless atmosphere that fosters a sense of calmness and tranquility. In Japandi interiors, neutral hues such as beige, gray, taupe, and off-white[1] dominate the color scheme, providing a versatile backdrop that allows other design elements to shine.

These soft, muted tones evoke a sense of warmth and coziness while maintaining a sense of sophistication and elegance. By avoiding bold or vibrant colors, Japandi style encourages a sense of visual continuity and unity throughout the space.

---

[1] Off-white is an umbrella term for a variety of shades that differ slightly from pure white, including cream, eggshell, vanilla, and ivory.

Color	Hex	RGB	Color	Hex	RGB
	#faf0e6	(250,240,230)		#d0c8b7	(208,200,183)
	#fff0db	(255,240,219)		#cbbfbf	(203,191,191)
	#eed9c4	(238,217,196)		#dcdad5	(220,218,213)
	#e4d5b7	(228,213,183)		#adabb2	(173,171,178)
	#d9b99b	(217,185,155)		#b7b7c9	(183,183,201)

A beige color palette on the left, a taupe color palette on the right

One of the key benefits of neutral hues is their ability to create a sense of spaciousness and openness. Light-colored walls and furnishings reflect natural light, making the space feel brighter and more expansive. This enhances the overall sense of tranquility and serenity within the home, creating an inviting atmosphere.

Neutral hues also provide a versatile foundation for layering textures and materials within the space. From smooth wooden surfaces to rough stone accents and soft fabric upholstery, neutral colors allow the tactile qualities of different materials to stand out. This adds depth and visual interest to the space while maintaining a cohesive and harmonious aesthetic.

Another advantage of using neutral hues is their ability to adapt to changing seasons and personal preferences. Unlike bold or trendy colors that may quickly become outdated, neutral tones have a timeless appeal that transcends temporary trends. This makes them an ideal choice for creating spaces that feel both contemporary and enduring, allowing you to enjoy your Japandi-inspired interior for many years to come.

Accent Colors & Their Significance

In Japandi interiors, accent colors are typically used sparingly to maintain the overall sense of simplicity and cohesion. They serve to punctuate the neutral color palette and draw attention to specific design elements or focal points within the space. Common accent colors in Japandi style include muted blues, greens, and earthy tones, which complement the soft, natural hues of the neutral backdrop.

Color	Hex	RGB	Color	Hex	RGB
	#562e19	(86,46,25)		#d8ebf6	(216,235,246)
	#9f6210	(159,98,16)		#849baa	(132,155,170)
	#79bedb	(121,190,219)		#8395c1	(131,149,193)
	#b4aa8d	(180,170,141)		#cba69e	(203,166,158)
	#e1d5b1	(225,213,177)		#435274	(67,82,116)

An earthy color palette on the left, a muted blues color palette on the right

The significance of accent colors in Japandi style lies in their ability to evoke specific moods or emotions within the space. For example, cool blues and greens can create a sense of tranquility and serenity, while warm earthy tones evoke a feeling of warmth and comfort.

In addition to adding visual interest, accent colors can serve a functional purpose. They can help define different zones within an open-plan layout, highlight architectural features, or create a sense of rhythm and flow throughout the space.

When selecting accent colors for a Japandi interior, it's important to consider the principles of balance and harmony that define the aesthetic. Colors should complement rather than compete with one another, creating a cohesive and unified look that feels intentional and thoughtfully curated.

By experimenting with different color combinations and observing how they interact with natural light and other design elements, you can find the perfect balance of hues to create a space that feels both tranquil and visually engaging.

Choosing the Right Color Palette

The sheer multitude of potential color combinations can be daunting when selecting a palette for your home or space. However, simplifying the decision to three colors can offer an effective starting point. This focused approach allows for easier matching of elements and ensures a cohesive aesthetic. This doesn't mean you can't introduce other colors, but by narrowing the scope, you will find it easier to match different elements. If you need help deciding on colors, it might help to review your wardrobe to see what colors fit your personal style and taste. For instance, maybe there's a specific color you like more than others that could form the base of your palette.

In implementing your chosen color palette, you might want to consider the *60-30-10 principle*, which is a popular guideline used in interior design for creating a balanced color scheme. It suggests dividing the colors in a room into three proportions: 60%, 30%, and 10%, each representing different roles within the space.

60% Dominant Color: This is the primary color that covers the largest portion of the room, typically the walls, floors, or large furniture pieces. The dominant color sets the foundation for the overall palette and establishes the room's mood. It's often a neutral or subdued hue that serves as a backdrop for other elements.

30% Secondary Color: The secondary color complements the dominant color and occupies about 30% of the space. This color adds visual interest and depth to the room, appearing in furniture upholstery, draperies, or accent walls. It should harmonize with the dominant color while providing contrast and variety. **10% Accent Color:** The accent color is the smallest portion of the scheme, making up around 10% of the room. It's used sparingly to add pops of color and personality, drawing attention to specific elements like throw pillows, artwork, or decorative accessories. This color provides contrast and visual excitement, tying the entire scheme together. In the case of Japandi style, examples of suitable accent colors include charcoal or a dark earthy green or brown.

In summary, following the 60-30-10 principle helps create a cohesive and balanced color scheme that allows for variation and interest while ensuring that the overall design remains unified and coordinated.

Texture Play: Mixing Soft & Hard Elements

Texture is another hallmark of Japandi style, adding depth, warmth, and tactile interest to interior spaces. Texture relates to the surface quality of any material, including visual and physical.

Visual textures are perceived through sight and can mimic the appearance of various materials, such as wood grain, stone patterns, or woven textiles, even if the surface is smooth to touch.

Physical texture refers to the tactile quality of a surface, which can be felt through touch and serves a vital role in adding depth, interest, and sensory richness to a space. In Japandi style, physical textures often include natural materials like wood, stone, bamboo, and rattan, which offer a tactile connection to the natural world. Examples include rough-hewn wooden furniture, smooth stone countertops, and woven rattan accents, which provide contrasting textures and contribute to the overall sensory experience of a room. Additionally, textiles like linen, cotton, and wool can introduce softness and warmth.

Texture play sometimes involves the deliberate mixing of soft and hard elements to create a dynamic and visually engaging environment. Soft textures, such as wool, linen, and cotton are often used for upholstery, curtains, and cushions, adding warmth and softness to furniture and décor accents. These textiles create inviting nooks and corners where you can relax and unwind.

Hard textures, on the other hand, provide contrast and structure to the space, adding visual interest and architectural detail. Materials such as wood, stone, and metal bring a sense of solidity and permanence to Japandi interiors, grounding the space and providing a strong foundation for the design. Wood is particularly prominent in Japandi style, with its natural grain and warm tones adding a sense of authenticity and connection to the natural world.

In Japandi interiors, the juxtaposition of soft and hard textures helps to create a sense of balance and harmony that is essential to the aesthetic. Smooth wooden surfaces contrast with soft fabric upholstery, while rough stone accents complement plush rugs and cushions. By mixing textures in this way, you can create spaces that feel layered and multidimensional, inviting everyone to explore and engage with their surroundings.

Another important aspect of texture play is the use of natural materials that celebrate the beauty of imperfection. Weathered wood, aged leather, and handcrafted ceramics add character and authenticity to the space, reflecting the passage of time and the unique history of each material. These imperfect textures create a sense of warmth and lived-in charm that is central to the appeal of Japandi interiors.

Chapter 5: Furniture & Furnishings

Functional Furniture Design

In Japandi interiors, form follows function, with every design decision driven by a desire to enhance the usability and livability of the space.

As discussed in Chapter 3, Japandi style favors furniture with clean lines and simple forms with a focus on essential features and minimal ornamentation. Moreover, each piece of furniture is carefully selected for its practicality, versatility, and ability to enhance the overall functionality of the space. To elaborate, furniture pieces may incorporate built-in storage compartments, hidden drawers, or multifunctional features that help to minimize clutter and maximize space efficiency.

This emphasis on functionality extends beyond standalone furniture to include permanent furniture such as built-in shelving, window seats, and hidden storage compartments. By integrating these functional elements seamlessly into the architectural design, Japandi furniture not only simplifies the visual appeal of the space but also contributes to a sense of organization and orderliness.

In addition to clean lines and functional design, Japandi style prioritizes modularity, offering flexibility and adaptability to changing needs. Modular furniture pieces can be easily rearranged, expanded, or adapted to suit changing needs and preferences. This flexibility allows you to customize your living spaces according to your lifestyle and the specific requirements of each room. Modular shelving units, for example, can be configured in various ways to accommodate different storage requirements and spatial constraints. These systems allow you to customize your storage solutions, whether that's for books, decorative objects, or multimedia equipment.

Sustainability and longevity

Sustainability and longevity are important aspects of furniture design in Japandi style. High-quality materials and craftsmanship ensure that furniture is built to last, reducing the need for frequent replacements and minimizing waste. Natural materials such as wood and leather are also used for furniture frames and upholstery, adding warmth and texture to the space while ensuring durability and longevity.

By investing in timeless pieces that are both durable and beautiful, you can create spaces that stand the test of time and continue to bring joy for years to come.

Choosing the Right Furniture

When it comes to find the right furniture for your home, the scale and proportion of furniture pieces should be carefully considered. Furniture should be scaled to fit the proportions of the room, creating a sense of balance and harmony within the space. Oversized furniture is avoided in favor of pieces that are appropriately sized for the room, allowing for ease of movement and circulation.

Comfort is another consideration. Upholstered seating features, plush cushions, and ergonomic designs all help to prioritize comfort without sacrificing style.

Finally, it's important to consider the shape of different furniture pieces. In general, Japandi shapes are inspired by nature with simple, organic, and clean lines following the principles of biomorphism, which bases artistic design elements on naturally occurring patterns or shapes reminiscent of nature and living organisms. An example of biomorphism is the Butterfly Stool, which emulates the wings of a butterfly.

The iconic Butterfly Stool, designed by Sori Yanagi in 1954, epitomizes the elegant simplicity of Japanese design. Crafted from a single curved plywood sheet, this minimalist yet ergonomic stool embraces the Japanese philosophy of emphasizing form and function. Its graceful silhouette, reminiscent of a butterfly's wings, seamlessly blends traditional craftsmanship with modern aesthetics.
www.vitra.com

Curved lines, exemplified by designs like the Butterfly Stool, integrate the natural aesthetic of Japandi and contribute a soft feel to the room while adding contrast to horizontal and vertical sight lines, which are more common.

Different types of lines contribute to the overall aesthetic and atmosphere of the space, working together to evoke a sense of cohesion and unity. From a design perspective, horizontal sight lines (parallel to the ground) invoke a sense of stability, groundedness, and calmness. They can be found in elements like furniture pieces, shelving, or architectural features such as moldings or countertops.

Vertical sight lines, meanwhile, rise perpendicular to the ground, adding a sense of height and grandeur to the room. They are often represented by features like tall cabinets, doorways, or floor-to-ceiling windows. Vertical lines draw the eye upward, creating an illusion of spaciousness and emphasizing the room's vertical dimensions.

Lastly, there are organic sight lines, such as curved lines, as already mentioned. Organic sight lines are inspired by natural forms like waves, clouds, or foliage. They help to bring a sense of movement and vitality to the space, softening the rigid geometry of horizontal and vertical lines. Organic lines can be found in furniture shapes, decorative accents, or architectural details such as arches or curved walls.

When combined, these three types of sight lines help to create a visually engaging and balanced environment.

Incorporating Japanese & Scandinavian Pieces

In Japandi style, furniture and furnishings are carefully chosen to reflect the sharing of design sensibilities. This fusion results in interiors that are both functional and aesthetically pleasing, with each piece contributing to the overall harmony and balance of the space.

Japanese furniture is characterized by its simplicity, craftsmanship, and connection to nature. Traditional Japanese pieces such as tatami mats, low tables (known as a chabudai in Japanese) with short table legs used for tea or dining, and sliding doors bring a sense of authenticity and tranquility to Japandi interiors. These pieces are mostly made from natural materials such as wood, bamboo, and rice paper, reflecting a reverence for the natural world and the beauty of imperfection.

Japanese-style low table known as a chabudai

In traditional Japanese homes, it was common for family members to sit on tatami mats made from woven rush straw, which provides a soft, gentle springiness. These mats provide a comfortable base for cushions (including traditional zabuton cushions) and futon mattresses. Note that although tatami mats were ubiquitous in most Japanese homes until recent decades, wooden and carpeted floors have gradually replaced them in most modern homes.

Scandinavian furniture, meanwhile, is known for its clean lines, minimalist aesthetic, and focus on functionality. Pieces such as Danish teak furniture and Swedish Gustavian chairs bring a sense of modern elegance and simplicity to Japandi interiors. (Danish teak refers to a tropical hardwood known for its durability, resistance to rot, and attractive grain patterns. Danish designers favor teak for its rich, warm color and ability to be sculpted into sleek, modern forms.)

Beyond teak furniture, Scandinavian furniture often features light-colored woods, sleek silhouettes, and modular designs that emphasize usability and versatility.

Pair of Gustavian white armchairs, Sweden Circa 1910

When incorporating Japanese and Scandinavian pieces, it's important to strike a balance between the two design traditions. This can be achieved by selecting furniture items that share common characteristics, such as clean lines, natural materials, and a focus on craftsmanship. Mixing and matching Japanese and Scandinavian pieces can also add visual interest and depth to the space, creating a dynamic and layered aesthetic.

Ultimately, incorporating Japanese and Scandinavian pieces is about embracing the principles of simplicity, functionality, and natural beauty. Whether it's a Japanese shoji screen or a Scandinavian mid-century armchair, each piece should contribute to the overall harmony and balance of the space.

Multi-functional Pieces & Small Spaces

In Japandi style, where simplicity and functionality are paramount, multi-functional furniture pieces play a crucial role, especially in smaller living spaces. These pieces are designed to maximize usability, space, and versatility without compromising on style, making them ideal for modern urban dwellings where space comes at a premium.

Furniture with low legs or close to the floor, for example, can help to enhance the feeling of space in a room, which is why you will often see Japanese furniture in small-sized rooms sitting close to the floor.

Multi-functional furniture, meanwhile, can help to reduce the need for multiple pieces of furniture. The futon sofa bed is a typical example with this versatile piece serving as both a comfortable seating option during the day and a cozy bed for overnight guests.

Futons are generally lightweight and easy to move around, making them a convenient option for those who prefer to rearrange their sleeping space or put it out of sight during the day. Additionally, futon covers are removable and washable, facilitating easy maintenance and hygiene.

Japanese futon on a low wooden frame

Convertible dining tables are another practical solution for small living spaces. These tables can be expanded or collapsed as needed, making them perfect for everyday meals and larger gatherings. Some convertible dining tables even feature built-in storage compartments or adjustable heights, further maximizing functionality and usability.

In addition to multi-functional furniture pieces, small spaces benefit from smart storage solutions and space-saving design ideas. Wall-mounted shelves, under-bed storage bins, and fold-down desks are just a few examples of how to make the most of limited square footage without sacrificing style or comfort. More smart storage solutions are also discussed in the next chapter.

The next important aspect of Japanese interiors is adaptability. For instance, by using sliding doors called fusuma (also used as artistic canvases for painters), a large room can be converted into separate rooms. Shoji is another type of Japanese sliding door or screen, made of translucent paper on a wooden frame. They give a degree of privacy while also allowing soft natural light to flow into the room.

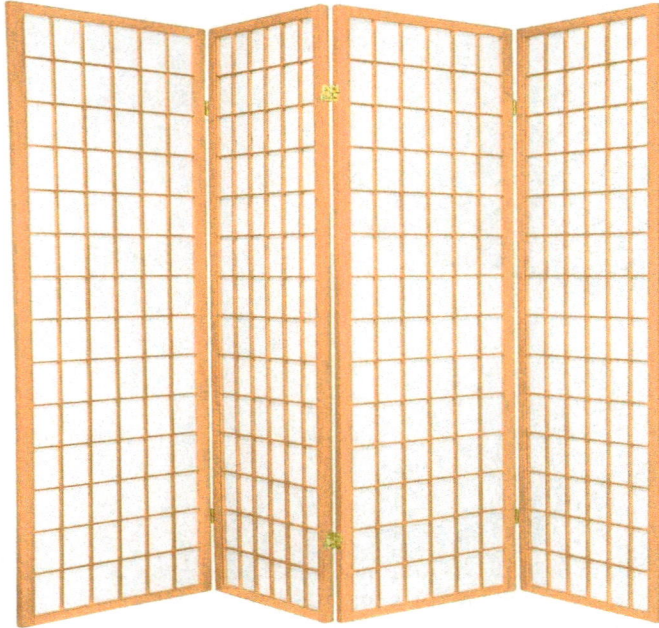
Shoji screens

A more elaborate option is the Yukimi shoji, which comes with a sliding panel as its base, behind which is a sheet of glass. This type of screen allows you to stay warm inside while viewing the winter scene outside. Yukimi literally means "snow viewing" in Japanese.

Yukimi shoji

Japandi Furniture Outlets

The following are some noteworthy outlets where you can find and acquire exquisite Japandi furniture pieces.

Anthropologie: Blending the rustic charm of Bohemian style with the clean lines and simplicity of Japandi, you will see that Anthropologie offers a Japandi aesthetic in many of their collections.

Ariake: Crafting elegant furniture pieces inspired by Japanese craftsmanship, Ariake offers collections that fit the Japandi aesthetic.

Article: Known for its sleek lines and functionality, this direct-to-consumer brand offers a range of modular and neutral offerings.

Blu Dot: Known for modern, affordable furniture ideal for small spaces, Blu Dot's designs are sleek and contemporary, aligning well with the minimalist side of Japandi.

Cisco Home: This brand provides environmentally-friendly furniture with a focus on handcrafted quality and comfort, aligning well with the Japandi philosophy of sustainable and timeless design.

Fritz Hansen: Renowned for its iconic designs and commitment to quality craftsmanship, Fritz Hansen's modern furniture pieces complement the Scandinavian side of Japandi.

Hay: This Danish company offers Scandi-inspired simplistic pieces. Their furniture combines modern design with practicality.

Gray Pants: Offers unique lighting and furniture with an emphasis on sustainable design. Their pieces often have a sculptural quality that can add interest to a Japandi space.

IKEA: Known for its Scandinavian traditional and modern lines, IKEA offers a range of furniture offering functionality and simplicity.

Industry West: Offers a range of mid-century and Japandi-inspired furnishings. Their pieces often combine rustic elements with modern design.

Kasala: An Indonesian brand focusing on rattan and teak wood furniture. These natural materials are ideal for adding warmth and texture to a Japandi-styled home.

Les Jardins: Specializing in outdoor furniture with a sustainable approach, Les Jardines helps bring a natural, Japandi aesthetic into outdoor spaces.

Lintex: Known for its innovative solutions in functional furniture and interior design, this Swedish brand offers products that harmonize well with the Japandi style, focusing on simplicity and utility.

MUJI: Renowned for its minimalist and functional designs, this iconic Japanese brand emphasizes simplicity in its products and is perfect for creating a serene space.

Open Spaces: Specializing in Japanese-influenced organizational furniture, Open Space furniture products are great for creating clean, clutter-free spaces.

Takt: Takt specializes in sustainable and minimalist furniture designs, offering pieces that embody the simplicity and functionality central to Danish design.

Plint: This table, designed by Danish brand Takt, can serve as a coffee table in front of the sofa, as a side table against the wall or beneath a window, as a bench in the entrance for putting on your shoes, or merely as a platform for books and papers. The table can be quickly and easily folded down when you need to save space and then reassembled with no need for glue, bolts, or screws.
taktcph.com

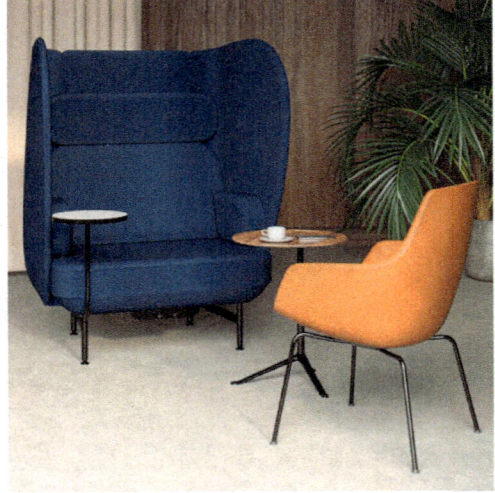

Little Friend: Produced by Danish brand Fritz Hansen, this portable and adjustable side table provides a perfect surface for your morning coffee or laptop as you work from the sofa or a comfortable lounge chair.
fritzhansen.com

Air Whiteboard: This Swedish whiteboard from Lintex introduces a light beige color. Lintex's Air Whiteboard series provides an alternative to a traditional frame, creating a sense that the board is floating on the wall.

lintex.se

Kata Coat Stand: Designed by the Japanese furniture brand Ariake, this unique coat stand provides a handy place to hang your coat and store your shoes. While large, its proportions are inspired by Japan's traditional Kimono stand, which makes for an interesting talking point when welcoming guests.

ariakecollection.com

Wood Linen: This premium Swedish noticeboard combines a solid oak frame with a natural linen surface suitable for pinning newspaper cutouts, notes, and other items.
lintex.com

The Wishbone Chair: Designed in 1949, the Wishbone Chair is an iconic masterpiece of Danish design. Crafted from solid wood, this chair exemplifies the Danish emphasis on craftsmanship, functionality, and organic forms. The hundred steps required to make a Wishbone chair are mostly done by hand. Its distinctive Y-shaped backsplat and graceful lines help create a harmonious blend of strength and elegance.

www.carlhansen.com

Chapter 6: Spatial Layout & Organization

Open Floor Plans: Maximizing Space & Light

Open floor plans are a common feature of Japandi, reflecting the minimalist principles of Japanese and Scandinavian design traditions. By removing barriers and partitions between living spaces, open floor plans create a sense of flow, spaciousness, and connectivity within the home.

One of the key benefits of open floor plans is their ability to maximize natural light and ventilation throughout the space. Without walls or partitions to block the flow of light, natural sunlight can penetrate deeper into the interior, creating bright and airy living spaces. This not only enhances the visual appeal of the space but also reduces the need for artificial lighting during the day, contributing to energy efficiency and sustainability.

In addition to maximizing space and light, open floor plans foster a sense of social interaction and connectivity within the home. Without barriers to separate occupants, family members and guests can easily engage in conversation and shared activities, promoting a sense of togetherness and community.

In Japandi-style open floor plans, the layout of furniture and furnishings is carefully considered to maintain a sense of balance and harmony within the space. Furniture is arranged to define different zones or areas within the open plan, such as a seating area, dining area, or workspace. This creates visual continuity and cohesion while allowing each area to retain its unique identity and purpose.

By arranging furniture in a way that encourages circulation and openness, you can maximize the usability and functionality of the open floor plan while creating living spaces that feel spacious and inviting.

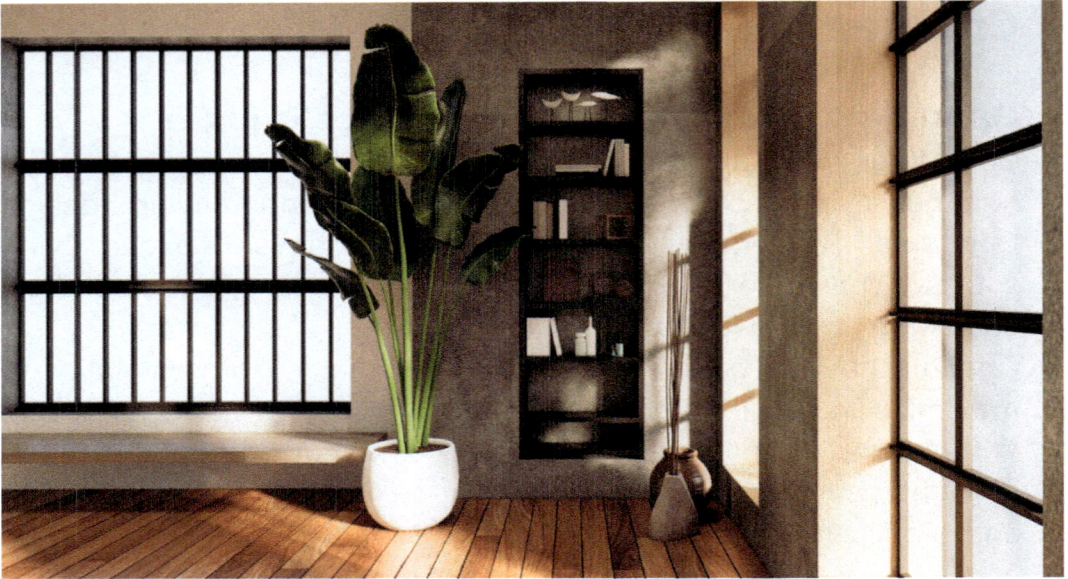

Minimalistic Storage Solutions

In Japandi style, minimalistic storage solutions play a crucial role in maintaining the clean and clutter-free aesthetic of the interior while maximizing functionality and usability. These storage solutions are designed to be both practical and visually appealing, seamlessly integrating into the overall design of the space.

One of the key principles of minimalistic storage solutions in Japandi style is the use of built-in storage wherever possible. Built-in shelves, cabinets, and closets are typically integrated into the architecture of the space, providing discreet storage options that blend seamlessly with the surrounding walls and surfaces. This helps to minimize visual clutter and maintain a sense of openness and simplicity within the home.

Another common feature of minimalistic storage solutions in Japandi interiors is the use of multi-functional furniture with built-in storage compartments. Ottoman benches with hidden storage, coffee tables with lift-top lids, and bed frames with drawers underneath are just a few examples of how furniture can serve dual purposes while still providing additional storage space. These multi-functional pieces help to maximize space efficiency and reduce the need for standalone storage furniture. Ottoman benches, for example, can serve as a comfortable footrest and as a discreet storage solution for blankets, pillows, and other items. Some storage ottomans even feature removable trays or lids, allowing them to double as coffee tables or extra seating when needed.

In addition to built-in storage and multi-functional furniture, Japandi-style interiors often incorporate clever organizational solutions to keep belongings tidy and accessible. Drawer dividers, closet organizers, and wall-mounted hooks and racks help to maximize the efficiency of storage spaces and make it easier to stay organized.

When it comes to material choices for minimalistic storage solutions, natural materials such as wood, bamboo, and rattan are preferred for their warmth, durability, and visual appeal.

Overall, minimalistic storage solutions help to maximize space efficiency, reduce visual clutter, and promote a sense of calm and orderliness within the home, reflecting the core principles of Japandi design.

Creating Zen Zones: Meditation & Relaxation Spaces

In Japandi-style interiors, creating designated Zen zones for meditation and relaxation can be highly effective in promoting a sense of tranquility and well-being within the home. These dedicated spaces provide opportunities for introspection, mindfulness, and rejuvenation, allowing you to escape the stresses of daily life and reconnect with your inner sense of calm.

When designing a meditation corner or relaxation space in a Japandi-style interior, it's important to prioritize simplicity, comfort, and serenity. Start by selecting a quiet and peaceful corner of the home where distractions are minimal, such as near a window with a view of nature or in a secluded alcove away from high-traffic areas of the home.

Once you've chosen the location, consider the layout and furnishings of the space. Keep the design clean and uncluttered, with minimal furniture and décor that promotes a sense of openness and tranquility. A comfortable meditation cushion or chair, a small side table for candles or incense, and a soft rug or mat to define the space are all essential elements for creating a welcoming and inviting atmosphere.

Natural materials such as wood, bamboo, and stone can also help to enhance the sense of serenity and connection to nature within the meditation corner or relaxation space. Consider incorporating these materials into the design through furniture, décor accents, or flooring to create a sense of warmth and authenticity.

Soft lighting is another consideration. Opting for warm, diffused lighting sources such as floor lamps, table lamps, or string lights creates a soft and gentle ambiance that encourages relaxation and introspection. Avoid harsh overhead lighting or bright, glaring lights that can disrupt the sense of tranquility and calmness.

To further enhance the Zen-like atmosphere of the space, consider incorporating elements of nature into the design. A small indoor plant, a water feature such as a tabletop fountain, a Japanese rock garden, or natural artwork inspired by landscapes can all evoke a sense of serenity and connection to the natural world.

Lastly, consider adding personal touches and meaningful elements to the space that resonate with your sense of spirituality or well-being. This could include religious or spiritual artifacts, inspirational quotes or artwork, or personal mementos that bring a sense of comfort and peace to the space.

.

Chapter 7: Lighting Design

Japandi is all about achieving a harmonious and serene ambiance and which leads us to the important role of lighting. Both Japanese and Scandinavian design traditions place a strong emphasis on celebrating and incorporating natural light. However, when natural light is scarce, clever and intentional lighting becomes essential in creating the desired atmosphere.

In traditional Japanese homes, the andon, a handcrafted lamp made from materials like paper, bamboo, wood, or metal, was one common source of light. These ingenious lighting fixtures provided just the right amount of illumination to navigate the night without disrupting the tranquil ambiance. Similarly, in Scandinavia, the warmth of the hearth was the primary source of light until the introduction of candles in the 19th Century.

In modern Japandi interiors, lighting is meticulously considered to evoke a sense of calm and coziness. Strategically placed floor lamps, table lamps, and overhead lighting work in harmony to create a layered, warm, and inviting atmosphere. Natural materials like wood, paper, and textiles are often incorporated into the lighting fixtures, paying homage to the traditional andon and Scandinavian craftsmanship.

Soft, diffused lighting is also key in Japandi spaces, as it mimics the gentle glow of natural light and creates a soothing ambiance. Dimmers and warm-toned bulbs are essential for achieving this effect, allowing you to adjust the lighting to suit the mood and time of day. Candlelight, a nod to Scandinavian traditions, can also be incorporated to add a cozy, flickering warmth to the space.

In addition to ambient lighting, task lighting may need to be considered too. Well-placed reading lamps or focused natural lighting not only provide functional illumination but also create pockets of warmth and visual interest within the room.

Natural Light: Harnessing Sunlight

In Japandi-style interiors, natural light is considered one of the most important design elements, as it not only illuminates the space but also enhances the overall atmosphere and mood. Harnessing sunlight effectively, for instance, can create a bright, airy, and welcoming environment.

When designing a Japandi-style interior, maximizing the amount of natural light entering the space is crucial. Start by evaluating the layout of your home or space and identifying areas where natural light is abundant, such as windows, skylights, or glass doors. These openings should be kept unobstructed to allow sunlight to flood into the interior, creating a sense of spaciousness and connection to the outdoors.

To optimize the impact of natural light, consider the placement of furniture and décor within the space. Positioning reflective surfaces such as mirrors or light-colored walls near windows can help to bounce sunlight deeper into the room, enhancing brightness and reducing the need for artificial lighting during the day. Avoid heavy drapes or window treatments that block sunlight and opt instead for sheer curtains or blinds that filter light while maintaining privacy.

In addition to enhancing brightness, natural light has a profound effect on the color and texture of materials within a space. Warm sunlight can accentuate the natural grain of wood, highlight the texture of textiles, and bring out the subtle hues of décor accents. By embracing these natural variations, you can create a dynamic and inviting atmosphere that evolves throughout the day as the angle and intensity of sunlight changes.

When designing lighting schemes for Japandi-style interiors, it's important to prioritize flexibility and adaptability to changing daylight conditions. Incorporating adjustable lighting fixtures such as dimmer switches or task lamps allows you to tailor the lighting levels according to your specific needs and preferences, whether that's for reading, working, or relaxing. This flexibility helps to create a versatile and comfortable environment that can easily transition from day to night.

Ambient Lighting for Warmth & Comfort

Ambient lighting plays a vital role in creating a warm, comfortable, and inviting atmosphere. Unlike harsh overhead lighting, ambient lighting is soft and diffused, providing gentle illumination that enhances the overall mood and ambiance of the space.

One of the key principles of ambient lighting is to avoid direct glare or harsh shadows. Instead, opt for indirect lighting sources such as wall sconces, floor lamps, or pendant lights that cast a soft, even glow throughout the room. These fixtures help to distribute light more evenly, creating a sense of warmth and coziness that encourages relaxation and comfort.

When selecting ambient lighting fixtures for a Japandi-style interior, consider the scale and proportion of the space. Choose fixtures that are appropriately sized for the room, taking into account the height of the ceilings and the overall layout of the furniture. Oversized fixtures can overwhelm smaller spaces, while undersized fixtures may not provide enough light to illuminate larger rooms.

In addition to selecting the right fixtures, pay attention to the color temperature of the light emitted by the bulbs. Warm white or soft white bulbs are ideal for creating a cozy and inviting atmosphere, while cooler color temperatures can feel too harsh and clinical. **Light bulbs with a warm color temperature (ideally 2700K to 3000K) are ideal.** Alternatively, consider using dimmable bulbs or fixtures with adjustable color temperatures to create the perfect ambiance for different activities and times of day.

Layering ambient lighting with other types of lighting, such as task lighting and accent lighting, also helps to create depth and dimension within the space. For example, combining ambient lighting with focused task lighting in work areas or reading nooks provides the perfect balance of overall illumination and localized brightness. Similarly, adding accent lighting to highlight architectural features or decorative elements adds visual interest and drama to the interior. Note that accent lighting is usually brighter than decorative lighting.

Another important consideration is how you integrate fixtures into the overall design scheme. Ideally, you want to choose fixtures that complement the aesthetic of the space, whether it's minimalist and modern or rustic and organic. Considering the materials, finishes, and shapes of the fixtures therefore helps to ensure they harmonize with the rest of the décor.

Statement Lighting Fixtures

In Japandi-style interiors, statement lighting fixtures serve as focal points that add visual interest, personality, and sophistication to the space. These fixtures not only provide illumination but also serve as works of art, enhancing the overall aesthetic and ambiance of the interior.

Statement lighting fixtures come in a variety of styles, sizes, and materials, allowing you to choose the perfect fixture to suit your individual preferences. Whether it's a sleek and sculptural pendant light, a bold and geometric chandelier, or a rustic and industrial floor lamp, there are endless options available to create a striking focal point in the room.

When selecting statement lighting fixtures for a Japandi-style interior, consider the overall design theme and mood of the space. Choose fixtures that complement the minimalist aesthetic of Japanese and Scandinavian design traditions, while also adding a touch of modern elegance and sophistication. Look for fixtures with clean lines, simple shapes, and understated details that reflect the appeal of Japandi style.

The placement of statement lighting fixtures is also important for creating a balanced and harmonious composition within the space. Consider placing fixtures above key areas such as dining tables, kitchen islands, or seating areas to draw attention and create a sense of intimacy and focus. Alternatively, use statement lighting fixtures to highlight architectural features or decorative elements within the room, adding depth and dimension to the interior.

In addition to their visual impact, statement lighting fixtures contribute to the overall functionality and usability of the space. Consider the type and quality of light emitted by the fixture, ensuring that it provides adequate illumination for the intended purpose.

Whether it's ambient lighting for general illumination or task lighting for specific activities, it's best to choose fixtures that meet the lighting needs of the room while also making a bold design statement.

PH 5 Pendant: The PH 5 Pendant light, designed by the legendary Poul Henningsen in 1958, is an iconic masterpiece of Danish lighting design. Henningsen's pioneering work on the study of light behavior and his pursuit of creating the perfect lighting solution culminated in the PH 5's unique design. Crafted with a sophisticated layering of curved metal shades, the PH 5 is engineered to precisely sculpt and direct light to create a warm, glare-free illumination.

www.louispoulsen.com

Verner Panton Light: Designed by the iconic Danish designer Verner Panton in 1964, this visually striking lighting fixture instantly challenged traditional design conventions. Its futuristic, organic shape was a radical departure from the straight lines and geometric forms that dominated mid-century design, embodying the spirit of the 1960s counterculture and experimentation. Crafted from spiral-shaped lacquered metal and acrylic panels, it not only illuminates a space but also serves as a striking piece of art, transforming the environment with its mesmerizing luminosity.

www.lampemesteren.com

Chapter 8: Decorative Accents & Accessories

Japanese Inspired Décor

In Japandi-style interiors, incorporating Japanese-inspired décor elements helps to add depth, authenticity, and a sense of cultural richness to the space. These decorative accents pay homage to traditional Japanese design principles while also complementing the clean lines and minimalist aesthetic of Scandinavian style.

One iconic Japanese décor element commonly found in Japandi interiors is Ikebana, the art of Japanese flower arranging.

Ikebana, which translates to "living flowers" or "making flowers alive," is not just about creating aesthetically pleasing compositions but also about expressing the essence of the natural world and the human spirit through floral design. The practice is deeply rooted in Japanese philosophy and aesthetics, drawing inspiration from concepts such as wabi-sabi (the beauty of imperfection), mono no aware (the ephemeral nature of existence), and ma (the concept of negative space).

Unlike Western floral arrangement styles, which often prioritize fullness and symmetry, Ikebana embraces a more restrained approach, focusing on the inherent beauty of individual elements and the relationship between them. This takes the form of a three-pointed structure, which is used to represent humanity, the earth, and heaven. Elements are then carefully chosen, with most ikebana designs using 5-13 stems with ample spacing between stems.

Ikebana arrangements will often incorporate seasonal elements, such as living branches, leaves, blossoms, and grasses, to reflect the changing rhythms of nature and evoke a sense of connection to the natural world. Unlike Western floral arrangements, ikebana flowers do not have to be in bloom at the same time and these arrangements often include a bud to represent the promise of hope. Other materials you may like to include in your design are stones and moss.

Lastly, if you are wondering where to place your ikebana arrangement, you will find that the best place is usually an uncluttered space that draws natural attention. To learn more about ikebana, there are many resources available, including books, online tutorials, and workshops, that can provide guidance on the basic elements of Ikebana design, such as line, form, and balance. You can also consider joining a local Ikebana club or participating in online communities to connect with other enthusiasts.

Besides ikebana, shoji screens are another traditional Japanese design element that can add visual interest and versatility to an interior. As discussed earlier, these sliding paper screens are used to divide spaces, provide privacy, and filter light, while also adding a sense of elegance and sophistication to the interior. Shoji screens are often made from translucent paper stretched over a wooden frame, allowing soft, diffused light to filter through and create a warm and inviting ambiance.

In addition to Ikebana and shoji screens, there are many other Japanese-inspired décor elements that can enhance the overall aesthetic. These may include bonsai trees, lanterns, traditional ceramics, calligraphy artwork, or a floor chair.

Above is an example of a Japanese floor chair, known as a "tatami zaisu" in Japanese. You can usually find this type of chair on Amazon for around $60-80 USD. With a normal chair back and no legs, these chairs are surprisingly comfortable and ideal for reading, resting, and meditating. It's also possible to place two or more of these chairs around a low wooden table to create a communal area for chatting and drinking tea.

Tatami mats are also common. Made from woven straw, rice straw, or rush grass, these mats are known for their natural texture, durability, and ability to create a comfortable and cozy atmosphere within the home. In Japandi-style interiors, tatami mats are often used as floor coverings in living areas, bedrooms, and meditation spaces, adding a touch of authenticity and tradition to the interior.

Scandinavian Touches: Hygge-Inspired Comfort

In Japandi-style interiors, incorporating Scandinavian touches adds warmth, coziness, and a sense of hygge-inspired comfort to a space.

One hallmark of Scandinavian design often incorporated into Japandi-style interiors is the concept of hygge. Hygge-inspired touches add a sense of warmth and intimacy, making the space feel more inviting and conducive to relaxation and socializing.

One way to introduce hygge-inspired comfort is through the use of soft textiles and fabrics. Plush throws, cozy blankets, and soft cushions in natural materials such as wool, cotton, and linen add warmth and texture to the space. Layering textiles in different textures and tones also adds depth and visual interest, creating a sense of coziness and comfort that invites you to relax and unwind.

Another key element of hygge-inspired comfort is the use of warm, diffused lighting. Warm-toned light bulbs emit a soft, golden glow that enhances the sense of warmth and coziness, making the space feel more intimate and welcoming. Soft, ambient lighting sources such as table lamps, floor lamps, and string lights also create a gentle and inviting atmosphere.

In addition to textiles and lighting, incorporating natural materials and textures into the interior adds to the hygge-inspired comfort of the space. Choosing furniture and décor accents made from warm woods such as oak, birch, or walnut adds warmth and character to the room. You can also consider adding tactile elements such as sheepskin rugs, woven baskets, or ceramic pottery to enhance the sense of coziness and overall connection to nature.

Hygge-inspired comfort is also about creating spaces that promote relaxation and well-being, so consider adding cozy reading nooks with comfortable armchairs and ottomans too, or creating a cozy corner with a soft rug and floor cushions for lounging and socializing.

Incorporating Plants & Greenery

In Japandi-style interiors, incorporating plants and greenery is essential for adding warmth, vitality, and a connection to nature. Plants not only enhance the visual appeal of the interior but also contribute to improved air quality, increased productivity, and a sense of well-being.

When selecting plants for a Japandi-style interior, consider the overall aesthetic of the space and the specific lighting conditions of each room. Choose plants that thrive in low to moderate light conditions, such as snake plants, pothos, philodendrons, and peace lilies, for areas with limited natural light. For rooms with ample sunlight, consider plants that prefer bright, indirect light, such as succulents, spider plants, and rubber trees.

When it comes to choosing planters and containers, opt for minimalist designs that complement the clean lines and understated aesthetic of Japandi style. Choose neutral colors such as white, black, or earth tones, and select materials such as ceramic, terracotta, or wood that add warmth and texture to the space.

Next, consider mixing and matching different sizes and shapes of planters to create visual interest and variation within the interior while also invoking a more organic and natural look. You can also get creative by arranging plants strategically throughout the room to create focal points, soften hard surfaces, and define different areas within the interior.

Grouping plants together in clusters or arranging them in rows along windowsills or shelves helps to create visual continuity and cohesion while maximizing the impact of greenery within the space. Moreover, grouping plants allows them to grow better, creating their own microclimate. By clustering plants together, you can enhance air circulation around the foliage, promoting better ventilation and gas exchange. They also collectively release moisture through a process called transpiration. This increase in humidity is conducive to plant growth, especially for species that thrive in humid conditions. The higher humidity levels can help prevent moisture loss and reduce the risk of leaf desiccation, particularly in indoor environments with dry air.

In addition to traditional potted plants, consider incorporating other types of greenery such as hanging plants, trailing vines, or air plants to add vertical interest and dimension to the interior. Hanging plants suspended from ceiling hooks or wall-mounted planters create a sense of depth and movement within the space, while trailing vines cascading down bookshelves or countertops add a touch of whimsy and charm. Both options are useful if you want to keep the plant out of the reach of pets or young children. Finally, make sure you know where you want to place the plants before buying them. Different plants will thrive in different spots depending on the space, temperature, humidity, and light available, which makes it important to research each plant type before purchasing.

Chapter 9: Japandi Style in Different Rooms

In this chapter, we'll delve into the aesthetics of Japandi style room by room, applying the design principles discussed in previous chapters, starting with the living room.

While exploring various design inspirations, it's essential to acknowledge the reality that many of us are not starting with a clean slate or undergoing extensive renovations. Instead, we must work with what we have, embracing the challenge of infusing Japandi elements into existing spaces.

While we may not all have the luxury of starting from scratch, the following insights offer a glimpse into Japandi's full potential and what's possible.

The Living Room

The living room is often the focal point of a home, serving as a space for relaxation, entertainment, and socializing. In Japandi style living rooms, the design ethos of simplicity, functionality, and harmony is reflected in every aspect of the space. That said, it's important to be realistic about how you will utilize this room based on your needs and lifestyle. Depending on whether you have kids who need a place to play, pets who need a place to rest, or hobbies that take up space in the living room, you may need to break the rules from time to time. With this caveat in mind, let's review the common elements of designing a Japandi style living room.

Color Palette: Start by selecting a neutral color palette consisting of soft, earthy tones such as beige, taupe, gray, and white. These colors create a calming and cohesive backdrop for the rest of the design elements in the room.

Furniture: When it comes to furniture selection, go for pieces with clean lines, minimalist silhouettes, and functional design. Examples include low-profile sofas and armchairs with simple, streamlined frames, upholstered in natural fabrics such as linen or cotton. Other examples are multi-functional furniture pieces such as coffee tables with hidden storage, ottomans that double as extra seating, or modular shelving units that can be configured to fit the space.

Lighting: Incorporating statement lighting fixtures such as sculptural pendant lights, minimalist floor lamps, or sleek wall sconces adds visual interest and illumination to the living room. Layering lighting sources also creates a warm and inviting ambiance while combining ambient lighting with task lighting meets the needs of different activities and times of day.

Textiles: As the most hygge room in the house, adding soft textiles and cozy accessories can help to enhance the comfort and coziness of your living room. Don't be shy to layer plush rugs, textured throws, and cushions in warm tones to create inviting seating areas and cozy nooks for lounging and relaxation. Incorporating natural elements such as woven baskets, ceramic pottery, and decorative branches or stones can also bring a touch of the outdoors inside.

Greenery: Incorporating plants and greenery strategically throughout the living room helps to inject freshness, vitality, and a sense of tranquility. Choose low-maintenance plants such as succulents, snake plants, or pothos, and display them in stylish planters or hanging baskets to add vertical interest and dimension to the room.

Artwork: Feel free to personalize the space with meaningful artwork, photographs, or decorative objects that reflect your tastes and interests.

Low-profile Sofa: The centerpiece is a low-profile, light gray sofa that offers a modern and inviting look. Its clean lines and plush cushions emphasize comfort without sacrificing style.

Modern Coffee Table: In front of the sofa, there's a modern coffee table made from light wood. Its simple, rectangular design complements the minimalist aesthetic of the room.

Rug: Beneath the table and sofa, a woven rug adds texture and warmth to the space, inviting bare feet to enjoy its natural texture.

Ceramic Décor: Across the room, various ceramic pieces in neutral tones provide a decorative touch that's both artistic and understated.

Textile Accents: Soft textiles are present in the form of throw pillows and a cozy blanket on the sofa, adding comfort and a hint of color that harmonizes with the room's palette.

Side Seating: A knitted pouf offers additional seating or can serve as a footrest, contributing texture and functionality to the room.

Wooden Accents: A wooden side stand on the right introduces a natural wooden accent, reinforcing the connection to nature inherent in Japandi design.

Decorative Plants: A selection of plants in various pots introduces life and a splash of green, contrasting subtly with the wood and neutral colors in the room.

The Bedroom

The bedroom is a sanctuary for rest and relaxation, and in Japandi style bedrooms, the emphasis is on creating a serene and tranquil atmosphere that promotes restful sleep and rejuvenation.

Color Palette: Start by selecting a calming color palette consisting of soft, muted tones such as pale blues, greens, grays, and whites. These colors create a sense of serenity and tranquility, making the bedroom feel like a peaceful retreat. Avoid bold or vibrant colors, which can be overly stimulating and disrupt the sense of calmness in the space.

Furniture: Selecting furniture with clean lines, minimalist design, and natural materials creates a sense of simplicity and harmony in the bedroom. Consider opting for a low-profile bed frame made from wood or metal, paired with a comfortable mattress and simple bedding in natural fabrics such as cotton or linen. You can also incorporate storage solutions such as built-in closets, bedside tables with drawers, or under-bed storage boxes to keep the space organized and clutter-free.

Lighting: Using soft lighting sources such as bedside lamps, wall sconces, or pendant lights with dimmer switches creates a warm and inviting ambiance in the bedroom. Avoid harsh overhead lighting, which can be too bright and disruptive to sleep. Instead, use soft, diffused lighting to create a cozy and relaxing atmosphere.

Textiles: The bedroom is an ideal place to add layers of soft textiles and cozy accessories to enhance the comfort and warmth of the room. Layer plush rugs, textured throws, and cushions in complementary colors and patterns to create a cozy and inviting bed. Avoid overly ornate or heavy curtains, opting instead for lightweight fabrics and understated patterns to maintain the harmonious balance characteristic of Japandi style. Sheer or linen curtains in neutral tones can add softness and warmth while allowing natural light to filter through, enhancing the serene ambiance of the space. Alternatively, unadorned blinds made from natural materials such as bamboo or rattan can help to complement clean lines and organic textures in the bedroom.

Natural Elements: Incorporating natural elements such as indoor plants, wooden accents, and stone or ceramic décor brings a touch of the outdoors inside. Look for plants that thrive in low-light conditions such as peace lilies, ferns, or spider plants, and display them in stylish planters or hanging baskets to add life and vitality to the space.

Artwork: Personalize the bedroom with meaningful artwork, photographs, or decorative objects. Choose pieces that evoke a sense of calmness and serenity, such as nature-inspired artwork, soothing landscapes, or abstract prints in muted tones.

Finally, try to leave cables and electronic devices such as TVs, phones, and computers outside the bedroom.

Featured Room

Platform Bed: The centerpiece is a low wooden platform bed, embodying the simplicity of Japanese design and the practicality of Scandinavian style. It supports a mattress dressed in neutral-toned bedding, promoting rest and tranquility.

Bedding: The bedding choices are in soft linens, providing comfort and breathability, and a wool throw adds texture and warmth, an element often seen in cozy Scandinavian interiors.

Side Table: Next to the bed is a minimalist side table, which serves as a nightstand without cluttering the space.

Decorative Vases and Bowls: Above the bed on a ledge are ceramic vases and bowls in earthy tones. These provide a connection to natural elements and offer an understated decorative touch.

Artwork: The artwork above the bed is suggestive of a landscape, rendered in muted colors that complement the room's color scheme. This ties in with the Japanese practice of bringing the outside in and the Scandinavian appreciation for art inspired by nature.

Shoji Screen: A sliding shoji screen is present, serving as a wardrobe door. It adds cultural richness and practicality.

Plants: Greenery, through bonsai and potted plants, adds vitality and a touch of color. This living element is a nod to both cultures' love for incorporating nature into home decor.

Lighting: The room relies on natural lighting as well as ceiling lights along with a strategically placed bedside lamp that contributes to the room's peaceful ambiance.

Kitchen & Dining Area

The kitchen and dining area in a Japandi style home are designed to be functional, practical, and aesthetically pleasing spaces where meals are prepared, shared, and enjoyed together.

Color Palette: Start by selecting a neutral color, consisting of soft, earthy tones such as white, beige, gray, and natural wood. These colors create a clean and calming backdrop for the space, allowing the beauty of natural materials and textures to shine through.

Cabinets: Kitchen cabinets with clean lines, minimalist hardware, and ample storage help to keep the space organized and clutter-free. Opting for natural materials such as wood or bamboo for cabinet fronts, countertops, and flooring add warmth and texture to the room. Shelving or glass-fronted cabinets can be used to display dishes, glassware, and cookware, adding visual interest and personality to the space. Less visually pleasing items such as machines can be kept out of sight in a closed cabinet.

Cookware: In the Japandi kitchen, less is more. This means opting for minimalist cookware made from natural materials such as wood, ceramic, and cast iron. Consider sleek, unembellished pots and pans that prioritize functionality over ornamentation. A cast iron skillet and a ceramic rice cooker exemplify the perfect balance of form and function.

Serveware: Serve your culinary creations in style with organic serveware inspired by Japandi design principles. Choose handmade ceramic plates and bowls in muted earth tones or soft pastels. Embrace imperfection with irregular shapes and subtle textures that add character to your table setting. Wooden serving utensils complement the natural aesthetic, evoking a sense of warmth and authenticity.

Table Linens: Set a tranquil tone for your meals with simple yet elegant table linens. Opt for linen or cotton napkins and placemats in neutral shades such as beige, gray, or soft blue. Incorporate subtle patterns inspired by nature, such as delicate floral motifs or geometric designs reminiscent of Japanese origami. Keep table settings clean and uncluttered to create a serene dining experience.

Kitchen Tools: Efficiency is key in the Japandi kitchen, which means choosing functional kitchen tools that streamline meal preparation. Invest in high-quality knives with ergonomic wooden handles for precise slicing and dicing. Utilitarian gadgets like bamboo steamers and mortar-and-pestle sets add authenticity to your culinary arsenal while enhancing the overall aesthetic appeal of your kitchen space.

Storage Solutions: Maintain order in your kitchen with thoughtful storage solutions. Opt for open shelving made from natural wood or metal to showcase your minimalist cookware and serveware collections. Keep countertops clutter-free by storing essentials in stylish containers crafted from ceramic, glass, or bamboo. Embrace the concept of wabi-sabi, finding beauty in imperfection, by displaying well-loved kitchen tools with visible signs of use.

Greenery: As with other rooms, incorporating natural elements such as plants, herbs, or fresh flowers into the kitchen and dining area adds freshness, vitality, and a sense of connection to nature.

Sleek Cabinetry: The cabinetry, finished in light wood tones, offers a smooth, clean appearance. It's designed to maximize storage while maintaining a minimalist aesthetic, with handleless doors that emphasize a streamlined look.

Integrated High-End Appliances: Appliances are seamlessly integrated into the cabinetry, including a built-in oven, which contributes to the kitchen's sleek, uncluttered appearance.

Large Central Island: The central island serves multiple functions: as a preparation area, dining space, and social hub. The island also includes seating, with minimalist stools that tuck neatly under the overhang, providing a casual dining or workspace.

Minimalist Lighting Fixtures: Above the island, minimalist pendant lights offer targeted illumination without overwhelming the space. Their simple design complements the kitchen's overall aesthetic.

Natural Stone Countertops: The granite countertops provide a natural contrast to the light wood cabinetry. Their polished finish adds a sophisticated touch, while their natural patterning brings an organic element into the space.

Indoor Plants: Strategically placed indoor plants add a pop of greenery.

Hints of Black or Dark Gray Accents: Small details, such as the faucet, cabinet pulls, and light fixtures, are in black or dark gray. These accents provide a visual anchor, adding depth and contrast to the airy, light-filled space.

Bathroom

In a Japandi-style bathroom, the emphasis is on creating a serene and spa-like atmosphere promoting relaxation and rejuvenation. After all, both regions embrace the therapeutic benefits of water and the restorative power of relaxation, which is rooted in a shared cultural appreciation for bathhouses, hot springs, and sauna rituals.

Color Palette: Starting with the color palette, you should use a neutral color palette for the bathroom, consisting of soft, earthy tones such as white, beige, gray, and light wood. These colors create a sense of calmness and tranquility, making the bathroom feel like a peaceful retreat.

Fixtures: You may like to use matte or satin finishes for tiles, countertops, and cabinetry to create a cohesive look. For the vanity or countertop, consider one made from natural wood or stone, paired with a vessel sink or undermount sink for a clean and contemporary look.

Wash area: At the heart of the Japandi bathroom lies the bath or shower – the focal point of your at-home spa experience. If possible, embrace the simplicity of a walk-in shower or a frameless structure for an open and inviting ambiance. By eliminating barriers, you can invite a seamless transition and foster a sense of flow and openness. Also, consider installing a rain showerhead or handheld shower wand for a luxurious and spa-like experience.

Furniture: To maintain a clean and clutter-free aesthetic, conceal accessories within furniture units, keeping surfaces uncluttered and serene. This may mean adding storage solutions such as floating shelves, wall-mounted cabinets, or built-in niches to keep the space organized and clutter-free.

Lighting: Adding soft lighting sources such as wall sconces, vanity lights, or recessed lighting creates a warm and inviting ambiance in the bathroom. Avoid harsh overhead lighting, which can be too bright and disruptive to relaxation. Instead, use soft, diffused lighting to create a soothing and tranquil atmosphere that encourages relaxation and rejuvenation.

Natural Elements: Incorporating natural elements such as plants, bamboo accents, or decorative stones into the bathroom design brings a touch of the outdoors inside. It's advisable to select low-maintenance plants such as air plants or succulents and display them in stylish planters or hanging terrariums to add a pop of greenery and life to the space.

Artwork: You can personalize the bathroom with meaningful artwork, decorative objects, or personal touches. Here, you may like to add pieces that add warmth and personality to the space, such as framed photographs, ceramic pottery, or handmade textiles.

Freestanding Bathtub: A focal point in the room, this bathtub combines sleek, simple lines with ergonomic design.

Wooden Vanity with Vessel Sink: The vanity is minimalist in design with clean lines, constructed from natural wood to add warmth and texture. The vessel sink on top, in a contrasting material of ceramic, adds a modern touch that still respects the overall natural and minimalist theme.

Frameless Glass Shower Enclosure: This feature emphasizes openness and light, with a spacious design that minimizes visual clutter. The lack of frames and hardware aligns with the minimalist aspect of the Japandi style, making the bathroom feel larger and more cohesive.

Stone Flooring: The choice of stone for the flooring reinforces the connection to nature, providing a durable and tactile surface. Its natural variation in color and pattern adds depth and interest without overwhelming the space.

Seating: While not explicitly shown, Japandi style bathrooms sometimes include a small wooden stool or bench. These pieces are functional, offering a place to sit or to hold towels and bath products, and are made from natural materials to complement the room's aesthetic.

Storage Solutions: Simple, unobtrusive shelving and cabinets made from natural wood offer practical storage without sacrificing style.

Chapter 10: Bringing Japandi Style into Your Home

Tips for Japandi Style on Any Budget

Incorporating Japandi style into your home doesn't have to break the bank. Whether you're working with a tight budget or have more financial flexibility, there are plenty of ways to achieve the minimalist elegance and harmonious balance of Japandi design.

Start by decluttering and simplifying your space. Japandi is all about minimalism, so take the time to remove any unnecessary clutter or excess decor. Clearing out space will not only make your home feel more spacious and open but also allow the beauty of Japandi design to shine through.

Invest in key pieces of furniture that embody the principles of Japandi style. As mentioned throughout this book, look for pieces with clean lines, simple silhouettes, and natural materials such as wood, bamboo, or rattan. Focus on quality over quantity, choosing timeless pieces that will stand the test of time and complement the overall aesthetic of your home.

If you are looking to buy a new bed frame and mattress or replace an old one, opting for a Japanese futon will instantly save you money. While sleeping on the floor won't be a suitable option for all people due to physical considerations, people who sleep on a futon often cite enhanced spinal positioning and reduced back pain. If you are worried about the thickness of the futon, opt for a 10cm (3.9 inches) or a thicker futon rather than the standard 7cm (2.7 inches) thickness, which is more common in Japan.

Next, if purchasing new furniture is not an option, then consider repurposing or upcycling existing pieces to give them a fresh new look. Paint wooden furniture in neutral tones or reupholster cushions and upholstery in natural fabrics to create a cohesive and harmonious look that aligns with Japandi style.

Incorporating natural materials and textures into your décor will add warmth and depth to your space. Affordable options include woven baskets, ceramic pottery, or jute rugs that bring a touch of nature indoors. These simple yet stylish accents will enhance the overall aesthetic of your home and create a sense of tranquility and serenity.

When it comes to lighting, opt for affordable options like soft, diffused floor lamps or inexpensive string lights to create a cozy atmosphere without breaking the bank. Consider utilizing dimmer switches or affordable smart lighting solutions to adjust brightness levels according to your preferences.

To add greenery to your space without spending a fortune, choose low-cost, low-maintenance plants such as affordable succulents or snake plants. Display them creatively in budget-friendly planters or repurpose items like mason jars for a charming touch.

For a wallet-friendly finishing touch, focus on affordable minimalist accessories like thrifted ceramic vases, budget-friendly linen cushions, or DIY wooden trays. You can also experiment with affordable textures and materials to achieve depth and balance in your Japandi-inspired space without overspending.

By following these tips and incorporating Japandi-inspired elements into your home, you can create a stylish and harmonious living space that reflects your tastes and preferences based on your budget.

DIY Projects & Home Improvement Ideas

Embracing Japandi style in your home may not require a complete overhaul. With some creativity and DIY spirit, you can incorporate Japandi-inspired elements into your space through simple projects and home improvements.

One DIY project to consider is creating a minimalist gallery wall. You can start by selecting a few pieces of artwork or framed photographs that resonate with the serene and tranquil aesthetic of Japandi style. Choose simple frames in neutral tones and arrange the artwork in a cohesive layout on your wall. Experiment with different arrangements until you find one that feels balanced and harmonious, adding visual interest and personality to your space.

Another DIY idea is to update your furniture with a fresh coat of paint or new upholstery. Old wooden furniture can be given a modern makeover by painting it in a soft, muted tone such as white, gray, or beige. Alternatively, you can reupholster cushions and upholstery in natural fabrics such as linen or cotton. These simple updates can breathe new life into your furniture and give your space a fresh, updated look without breaking the bank.

Next, consider adding a touch of nature to your home with DIY planters and terrariums. Create stylish planters using materials such as ceramic pots, wooden crates, or woven baskets, and display them throughout your space to add life, color, and vitality. Alternatively, you can build your own terrariums using glass containers, pebbles, soil, and small plants such as succulents or air plants.

Upgrade your lighting fixtures with DIY pendant lights or sconces to create a warm and inviting atmosphere in your home. You can build your own pendant lights using materials such as wooden dowels, metal wire, or paper lanterns, and hang them above your dining table or kitchen island to create a focal point and enhance the ambiance of the space. Alternatively, you can install wall sconces with dimmer switches to provide soft, diffused lighting that can be adjusted according to your preferences. These DIY lighting projects add a touch of sophistication and elegance to your space while also enhancing the overall aesthetic.

Next, you may like to create a cozy and inviting atmosphere in your home with DIY textile projects such as cushions, throws, and curtains. Sew your own cushions using natural fabrics such as linen or cotton and fill them with soft, fluffy inserts for added comfort and style. Alternatively, you can knit or crochet your own throws using chunky yarns in neutral tones to add warmth and texture to your space. Finally, you can make your own curtains using light-filtering fabrics such as linen or sheer cotton.

These DIY textile projects add a personal touch to your home while enhancing comfort and coziness.

Finding Inspiration: Japandi Influencers & Designers

When it comes to embracing Japandi style in your home, finding inspiration from influencers and designers who specialize in this unique design aesthetic can be incredibly helpful. These individuals and brands offer valuable insights, tips, and ideas for incorporating Japandi-inspired elements into your space.

One influential figure in the Japandi design world is Kristina Dam, a Danish designer known for her clean lines, geometric shapes, and minimalist aesthetic. Dam's furniture and home accessories embody the principles of Japandi design, with their simple yet striking silhouettes and focus on quality craftsmanship. Follow Dam's work for inspiration on how to incorporate Scandinavian design elements such as sleek wood furniture, muted color palettes, and functional design into your space.

Social media platforms such as Instagram and Pinterest are other great sources of inspiration for Japandi style. Follow hashtags such as #japandi, #japandidesign, or #scandijapan to discover a wealth of images, ideas, and inspiration from designers, influencers, and fellow homeowners embracing this unique design aesthetic. You can also create mood boards, save images, and bookmark posts that resonate with you, and use them as a guide when decorating and styling your own home in the Japandi style.

In addition to individual designers and social media, there are several brands and companies that specialize in Japandi-inspired home décor and furnishings. MUJI offers a wide range of furniture, accessories, and household goods that are perfect for creating a Japandi-style home. Another brand to explore is IKEA, which offers affordable and stylish furniture and home accessories that embody the principles of Scandinavian design and are easily adaptable to the Japandi aesthetic.

Finally, don't be afraid to experiment and put your own spin on Japandi style. While it's important to draw inspiration from influencers and designers, ultimately, your home should reflect your own tastes, preferences, and personality. Mix and match different elements, experiment with textures and materials, and don't be afraid to break the rules and create a space that feels uniquely yours.

Chapter 11: Inspirational Spaces

Examples of Japandi Interiors

To appreciate Japandi style and its application in real-life settings, let's look at some stunning interiors that embody the fusion of Japanese and Scandinavian design.

In this large Kyoto apartment, traditional Japanese elements harmonize with Scandinavian minimalism. The living room features tatami mats adorning the floors and shoji screens delicately dividing the space, allowing soft natural light to permeate the room. Modern Scandinavian furniture pieces, characterized by their sleek lines and functionality, seamlessly integrate with traditional Japanese architecture. Throughout the apartment, plants are strategically placed to bring a touch of nature indoors, while subtle accessories add personality without overwhelming the serene atmosphere.

The following townhouse in Copenhagen showcases the blend of Scandinavian simplicity with Japanese aesthetics. Its bright and airy interior, adorned with white walls and pale wood floors, exudes warmth and tranquility. Traditional Japanese sliding doors and paper lanterns coexist harmoniously with Scandinavian design principles, maintaining a balance between functionality and elegance. Large windows and skylights flood the space with natural light, fostering a connection to the outdoors and enhancing the sense of serenity within.

Finally, this Stockholm loft epitomizes the fusion of Japanese and Scandinavian design sensibilities, creating a space that is both contemporary and inviting. Neutral tones dominate the color palette, while natural materials like wood, stone, and leather infuse warmth and texture into the interior. Clean lines and minimalist furnishings exude simplicity, while Japanese-inspired elements such as sliding doors and tatami mats add depth and cultural richness. With ample natural light streaming through expansive windows and skylights, the loft feels spacious and uplifting, further accentuating its Japandi charm.

Japandi in Commercial Spaces

Beyond residential spaces, Japandi is an excellent option for creating an inviting atmosphere for commercial spaces such as hotels, cafes, and other hospitality venues. Equally, Japandi's soothing qualities make it effective for offices, particularly open floor plans. Office furniture and accessories in Japandi style include desks, chairs, shelving, and storage that are minimal and timeless.

Finally, coworking spaces, cafes, yoga studios, and spas can incorporate Japandi elements to promote concentration and relaxation within their premises.

Fuglen Tokyo

As a renowned coffee shop and cocktail bar in Norway and Japan, Fuglen's multiple Tokyo locations offer a captivating blend of Scandinavian and Japanese design, creating a welcoming and culturally rich space where patrons can enjoy exceptional coffee, cocktails, and design in equal measure.

Fuglen Tokyo's location in Shibuya. Arrive before 10am to beat the mid-day rush!

Fuglen's Tokyo locations embody a harmonious fusion of mostly Scandinavian furniture and design influences with Japanese architecture, creating a unique and inviting space that pays homage to both cultures.

Situated in the large, bustling district of Shibuya, Fuglen Shibuya seamlessly integrates elements of mid-century Scandinavian design and furniture with Japanese aesthetics. The interior is characterized by clean lines, natural materials, and a warm color palette.

Upon entering Fuglen, patrons are greeted by a spacious and airy atmosphere, enhanced by abundant natural light streaming in through large windows. The interior is adorned with vintage

Scandinavian furniture, including iconic pieces by renowned designers such as Arne Jacobsen, Hans Wegner, and Finn Juhl. These meticulously curated furnishings contribute to the cozy and nostalgic ambiance, inviting patrons to relax and unwind in style. In addition to its Scandinavian furniture and design elements, Fuglen incorporates touches of Japanese craftsmanship including ceramics that add texture and depth to the decor.

Fuglen Tokyo's location in Shibuya doubles as a cocktail bar in the evening.

Famous Architects Embracing Japandi

Kengo Kuma: Renowned for his use of natural materials like wood and light, Kuma's buildings like the Yusuhara Wooden Art Museum and the Nezu Museum embody the Japandi spirit.

Jun Mitsui: Architect of the iconic Woodner apartment building in Washington D.C., Mitsui blends Japanese geometric patterns with American brickwork, creating a striking example of cross-cultural influence.

Nina Edwards Anker: As a Danish architect known for her calming and harmonious interiors, Anker incorporates elements of Japandi minimalism into her architectural projects, creating serene and functional spaces.

Norm Architects: This Danish studio's minimalist furniture and clean lines translate beautifully into architecture, evident in their projects like the Hotel Herman K in Copenhagen.

Ryue Nishizawa: Pritzker Prize-winning architect, Nishizawa's work like the White U and the Matsumoto House showcases a masterful blend of Japanese simplicity and contemporary functionality.

Yabu Pushelberg: A New York-based design firm known for its sophisticated and serene interiors, often blending Eastern and Western influences.

Chapter 12: Embracing Japandi Style in Your Life

Throughout this book, we have explored the key elements of Japandi style, from its origins and evolution to its practical applications in different rooms of the home.

From Tokyo apartments to Copenhagen townhouses to Stockholm lofts, these examples have provided valuable inspiration and insights into the versatility and adaptability of Japandi style. By drawing from the principles of simplicity and harmonious balance, you too can create spaces that feel both timeless and contemporary, elegant yet understated.

Whether you're looking to renovate your entire home or simply update a few key elements, incorporating Japandi style into your life can have a transformative effect on your living space. By prioritizing quality over quantity, embracing natural materials and textures, and creating a sense of openness and tranquility, you can cultivate a home environment that promotes relaxation, creativity, and well-being.

Remember, Japandi style is not just about aesthetics; it's about creating a lifestyle that aligns with your values and priorities.

Lastly, to help begin your journey, the following is a list of practical tips to help you get started today.

Practical Tips for Getting Started

1) Declutter: Japandi thrives on minimalism. This means every item should be carefully curated to celebrate the Japanese concept of danshari and retaining only the items you love.

One useful approach is to tidy room by room as this allows you to thoroughly examine every item in your home, one area at a time. This also enables you to identify and gather together all the objects that belong to a particular category as you progress through each room. By encountering and evaluating each item within a specific room, you can easily recognize and collect similar items scattered throughout that space. For instance, when tidying the living room, you may find various books, magazines, and reading materials that can be consolidated into one designated spot or category.

For further inspiration on this topic, see the Konmari Method made famous by Marie Kondo's breakout book (*The Life-Changing Magic of Tidying Up: The Japanese Art of Decluttering and Organizing*), or listen to *The Minimalists* podcast and watch their documentary on Netflix (*The Minimalists: Less is Now*).

2) Take an inventory: Begin by assessing your current inventory of furniture and ornaments to identify items that align with Japandi style. For example, look for pieces made of natural materials like wood, bamboo, or stone, and those with simple, clean lines. Next, use these items as a starting point for a redesign or rearrange them to create one room in the home dedicated to Japandi principles. Later, when you have more time and money to spend, you can start to update other rooms in the house.

3) Bring nature indoors: Incorporate elements of nature into your space. This could be through the use of plants or natural materials in your furniture and décor. Kokedama moss ball plants can help to capture the Japanese aesthetic while being more cost-effective and easier to maintain than most bonsai trees.

An example is the Meyer lemon tree kokedama, which costs US $140 from thekubode.com website. If you live in Japan, you can usually find similar versions for about US $30 at the plants section of Tokyu Hands.

4) Focus on functionality: Every item in your space should serve a purpose. You may also want to try and multitask when it comes to furniture, such as ottomans that store blankets or backless bar stools that slide under counters.

5) Choose understated wall art: When choosing your wall art, opt for simple, understated designs in neutral color palettes.

6) Use light wisely: Japandi design favors a seamless indoor/outdoor experience, with strong ties to the natural environment. This means that natural light should be allowed to circulate directly into your home as much as possible. At nighttime, candles can be strategically placed to provide soft, ambient lighting.

7) Value craftsmanship: Japandi style places value on the beauty of materials and quality of craftsmanship, so choose items that are well-made and will stand the test of time.

8) Create a cozy environment: Incorporate elements that promote coziness and comfort, such as soft textiles like plush rugs, throw blankets, and oversized floor cushions. Simply draping a blanket over the arm of the couch helps to add an extra touch of warmth and comfort to your living space. Additionally, you can introduce subtle lighting elements such as string lights or floor lamps to create a soft, inviting ambiance.

9) Add a Japanese touch: To infuse your space with a Japanese aesthetic, consider incorporating traditional elements such as shoji screens or sliding doors to divide spaces subtly. A tatami chair or low-slung seating with floor cushions can provide a comfortable and authentic touch. Minimalist Japanese artwork, such as a simple black and white ink painting or calligraphy, can add visual interest while maintaining simplicity. Lastly, incorporating a tatami mat area for meditation or relaxation provides a serene and traditional Japanese-inspired space within your home.

10) Enjoy the process: Don't chase perfection. Enjoy experimenting and let your Japandi style naturally evolve. The goal is to craft a peaceful space that inspires relaxation and well-being.

Recommended Resources

1. The Little Book of Hygge: The Danish Way to Live Well
by Meik Wiking
This book explores the Danish concept of "hygge," which is all about creating a warm atmosphere and enjoying the good things in life with good people. It's a guide to finding contentment and happiness in the simple things, emphasizing comfort, warmth, and togetherness.

2. The Life-Changing Magic of Tidying Up: The Japanese Art of Decluttering and Organizing by Marie Kondo
Marie Kondo's influential book introduces the KonMari method, a decluttering and organizing technique based on keeping only those things that speak to your heart and discarding the rest. It's a minimalist approach to possessions, aiming to enhance joy and serenity in living spaces.

3. Japandi Living: Japanese Tradition. Scandinavian Design.
by Laila Rietbergen
This book is a comprehensive guide to Japandi style, a blend of Japanese and Scandinavian design philosophies. It highlights how to create spaces that are simple, functional, and beautiful, emphasizing natural materials, clean lines, and a connection to nature.

4. Minimalism: A Documentary About the Important Things (Netflix Documentary)
Directed by Matt D'Avella, this documentary features Joshua Fields Millburn and Ryan Nicodemus, known as "The Minimalists," as they discuss minimalism as a lifestyle choice. The film explores how living with less can lead to more freedom, happiness, and meaning in life.

A simple and elegant New York apartment living room designed in the Japandi style. This space combines the best of Japanese minimalism and Scandinavian functionality, creating a serene and welcoming atmosphere with a focus on natural materials and simplicity.

A serene and functional work office. This space perfectly blends the minimalist aesthetics of Japanese design with the practicality and warmth of Scandinavian style, creating an inviting environment for work.

A modern and inviting man cave designed in the Japandi style. This space beautifully merges the functionality and warmth of Scandinavian design with the minimalist elegance of Japanese aesthetics, creating a cozy yet sophisticated retreat.